Dr Gareth Moore is the author of over 60 puzzle and brain-training books for both children and adults, including *The Mammoth Book of Brain Games, The Mammoth Book of New Sudoku* and *The Mammoth Book of Fun Brain Training*. His puzzles also appear in a range of newspapers and magazines, and he frequently features in the media as a puzzle expert.

He is also the creator of the daily brain-training website *BrainedUp.com*, and runs popular puzzle site *PuzzleMix.com*.

Also by Dr Gareth Moore

The Mindfulness Puzzle Book
The Mammoth Book of Logical Brain Games
The Mammoth Book of Brain Games
The Mammoth Book of New Sudoku
The Mammoth Book of Fun Brain Training
The Mammoth Book of Brain Workouts

Dr Gareth Moore

The Mindfulness Puzzle Book 2

ROBINSON

First published in Great Britain in 2017 by Robinson

1 3 5 7 9 10 8 6 4 2

A CIP catalogue record for this book
is available from the British Library.

ISBN: 978-1-47214-152-1

Typeset in Palatino Linotype by Dr Gareth Moore
Printed and bound in Great Britain by CPI Group (UK), Croydon
CR0 4YY

Papers used by Robinson are from well-managed forests and other responsible sources.

Robinson
An imprint of
Little, Brown Book Group
Carmelite House
50 Victoria Embankment
London EC4Y 0DZ

An Hachette UK Company
www.hachette.co.uk

www.littlebrown.co.uk

Contents

For Sara

Introduction

This second volume of restful puzzles and brain-training activities, designed to relieve stress and inspire creativity, features a refreshed range of specially selected games to provide the perfect level of challenge and reward for your brain. Feel the tension release as you focus on each achievable and fun task, and experience the endorphin reward buzz as you successfully complete each puzzle. What's more, all of the puzzles in this book have been specially created to provide a balanced level of challenge, meaning that you should be able to make good progress on virtually all of the puzzles.

Stimulating your mind with each puzzle also helps unlock your brain's innate creativity, just as sleep and rest can help you reach a breakthrough on pending tasks. This book will help you feel refreshed and renewed, and ready to carry on with your daily life. It also includes some special creativity and memory tasks, to help you to challenge your brain and practise these key skills.

The puzzles include a wide selection of classic puzzle types that you will be familiar with, as well as a small number of types that you might not have come across before. None of the puzzles have complex rules, however, so it's best to give them all a go, and let your brain enjoy the reward of successfully solving a new type of problem! There are also some more grown-up versions of childhood classics, with mindful activities such as colouring patterns, mazes, colour-by-number and even some creative drawing tasks.

Each puzzle should be solvable within a short break, so you don't need to set aside a lot of time to use this book. Just pick it up when you fancy a few minutes of mindful relaxation. And if you ever get stuck, just turn to the full solutions at the back to grab yourself a free hint!

So sit back, relax, and enjoy this second set of mindfulness puzzles.

Dr Gareth Moore – mindfulness@drgarethmoore.com

Floral Wordsearch

Can you find all of the listed flowers in the grid? Words are written forwards or backwards in any direction, including diagonally.

E	C	O	A	I	R	G	P	M	U	A	G	F	A	A
Z	A	L	A	I	A	O	A	R	M	G	L	A	A	R
L	P	A	R	G	L	R	S	A	N	Y	C	W	G	O
G	A	I	C	E	O	O	R	E	P	D	A	A	C	I
F	R	Z	L	D	W	Y	N	P	A	R	L	B	A	S
E	P	L	A	U	L	O	O	G	E	I	I	T	U	A
A	G	H	A	L	T	P	L	I	A	C	L	L	H	Y
A	A	D	I	R	E	I	A	F	A	M	O	B	Y	D
R	L	S	I	P	E	A	D	R	N	I	N	E	D	A
I	W	E	C	H	O	B	N	T	D	U	O	G	R	F
S	T	I	I	G	C	A	R	A	M	A	S	O	A	F
O	L	A	R	D	T	R	L	E	N	F	F	N	N	O
R	E	D	R	I	A	G	O	D	G	I	H	I	G	D
E	I	I	O	A	I	S	E	E	R	F	P	A	E	I
A	A	N	G	R	O	C	I	A	R	A	L	P	A	L

AMARYLLIS
AZALEA
BEGONIA
CARNATION
DAFFODIL
FREESIA
GERBERA
GLADIOLUS
HYDRANGEA
LILAC
MAGNOLIA
ORCHID
POPPY
ROSE
SUNFLOWER
TULIP

Heroic Heraldry

Using your imagination, can you use a pen or pencil to convert these blank images into pictures of four different **superhero capes**?

Link Words

Find a common English word to place in each gap, so that both when attached to the end of the first word and when attached to the start of the second word you end up with two more English words. For example, **birth** _ _ _ **break** could be solved using **day**, making **birthday** and **daybreak**.

space _ _ _ _ _ _ _ man

sigh _ _ _ _ _ mill

free _ _ _ _ cuffed

Island Mirage

Can you find the pair of identical islands? The remaining five illustrations each have slight differences from one another. The illustrations are rotated in order to provide a tougher challenge!

Letter Circle

How many words of three or more letters can you find in this letter circle? Each word should use the centre letter plus two or more of the other letters, and no letter can be used more than once in a single word. There is one word that uses every letter.

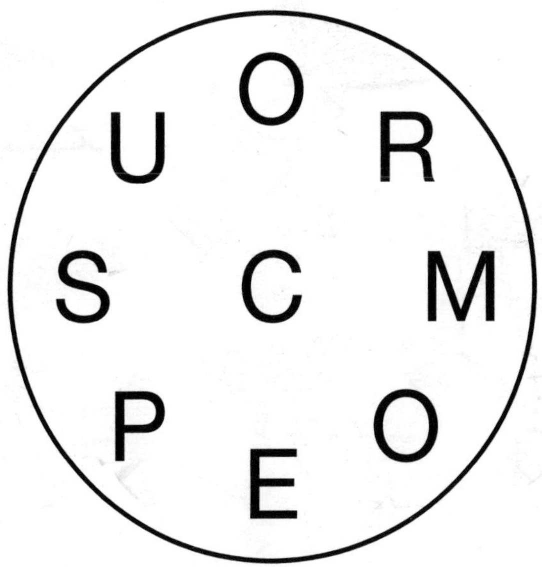

CORE SOURCE
COPE
CROP
COME
SCORE

Fancy a challenge? If so, can you find 50 words?

Missing Signs

Give your mind a workout by writing the missing mathematical sign into each of these equations: +, −, × or ÷.

1	+	57	=	58	43	+	17	=	60
29	+	1	=	28	11	+	42	=	53
10	×	5	=	50	12	+	11	=	23
71	+	20	=	91	24	−	12	=	12
5	÷	5	=	1	14	÷	7	=	2
5	×	9	=	45	10	×	9	=	90
12	×	4	=	48	15	÷	3	=	5
2	+	67	=	69	7	+	54	=	61
48	−	5	=	43	11	×	7	=	77
30	÷	6	=	5	44	−	8	=	36

Start and End

For each of these puzzles, add the same letter to both the start and end of the given fragment to form a normal English word. For example, add S to _TART_ to form STARTS.

_QU_

EPTET

MOEB

EURO

ULA

NCAS

_AW_

Mnemonic Memory

Using an acronym as a memory aid can really help with remembering a list of items. See if you can use the acronyms on this page, in the first letter of each column, to help you remember each of the words. Use the empty lists at the bottom of the page to see how you get on.

Decision	Indicate	Thought
Relaxation	Drifting	Hope
Excitement	Eagerness	Increase
Altogether	Aspiration	Nurture
Moment	Loving	Keen

______________	______________	______________
______________	______________	______________
______________	______________	______________
______________	______________	______________
______________	______________	______________

Types of Plant

Can you find all of the listed types of plant in the grid? They are written forwards or backwards in any direction, including diagonally.

```
T U E H S C N N S L C E U S B
L L R S N E E E A H R E T M U
U L A F S E R R S E W E C H R
B R E S G N A F B S L S H E H
G N O H I B W M N B V N U L S
H M F S U N I E A C M R E N R
U T E S R L R T A R F P E R N
S R H E C M E C O A E E E E I
B E F L B G T I R R R E N W L
L C A E E U L S E G R U I O V
D E I V S I B N R C D U V L R
B R E F C N N E U L E R T F I
R B C H S I V T R E E S R G L
R E E E A E E V S R W H E R B
W N S L T I L E S C E A L R W
```

BUSH
CACTUS
CLIMBER
EVERGREEN
FERN
FLOWER
GRASS
HERB
LICHEN
MOSS
PERENNIAL
SHRUB
TREE
VEGETABLE
VINE
WEED

Bridges

Draw horizontal and vertical lines to represent bridges joining these numbered islands. Bridges can't cross over either each other or another island, and you must build the bridges in such a way that you could travel from one island to any other using just the bridges. There can be no more than one bridge between any given pair of islands, and each island must have the given number of bridges connected to it.

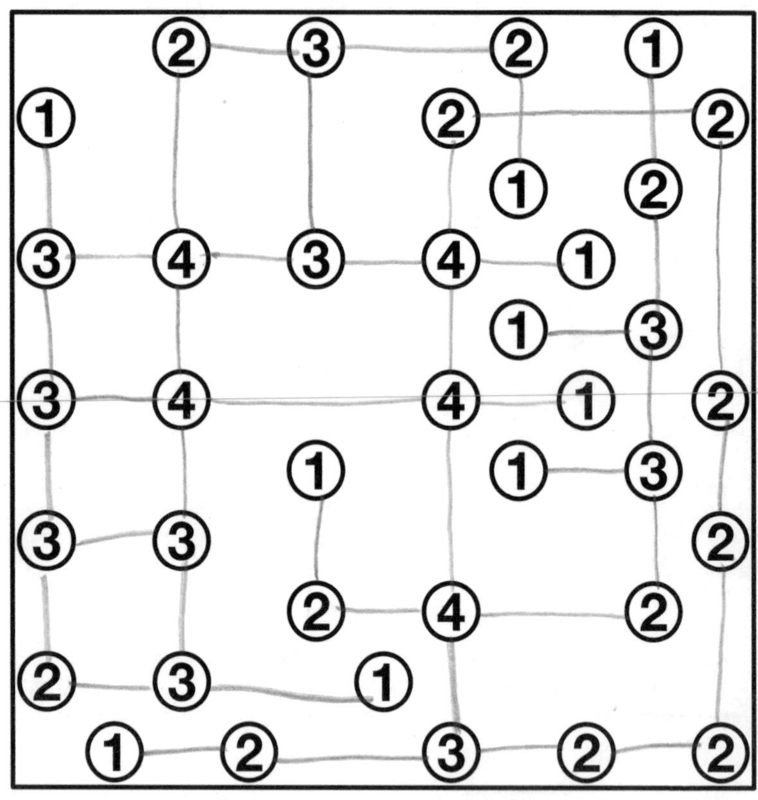

Simple Sudoku

See how quickly you can complete these easy puzzles – just place the digits from 1 to 4 into every row, column and 2×2 box for each puzzle.

Puzzle 1

4		3	
	1		2

Puzzle 2

	4		1
1		2	

Puzzle 3

	4		
		3	
	3		
		1	

Puzzle 4

3		2	
	1		4

Brain Chains

Can you solve each of the three brain chains completely in your head, without making any written notes? Start with the bold number at the top, and then apply each maths operation in turn. Write your final result in at the bottom.

39	**80**	**489**
÷3	-39	+130
-9	+77	-177
÷2	÷2	÷13
+50%	-30	+466
+19	+17	×3/5
RESULT	**RESULT**	**RESULT**
21	46	

Furnishing Decorations

Each of the following phrases can be rearranged to form an item of furnishing. Can you solve them all?

DEAD BIROS

BARE WORD

RUIN CAT

NICE BAT

SOLO OF TOT

3D Star Sudoku

Place 1 to 8 once each into every row, column and marked rectangle. Note that each row has one bend in it, as it travels over the 3D surface.

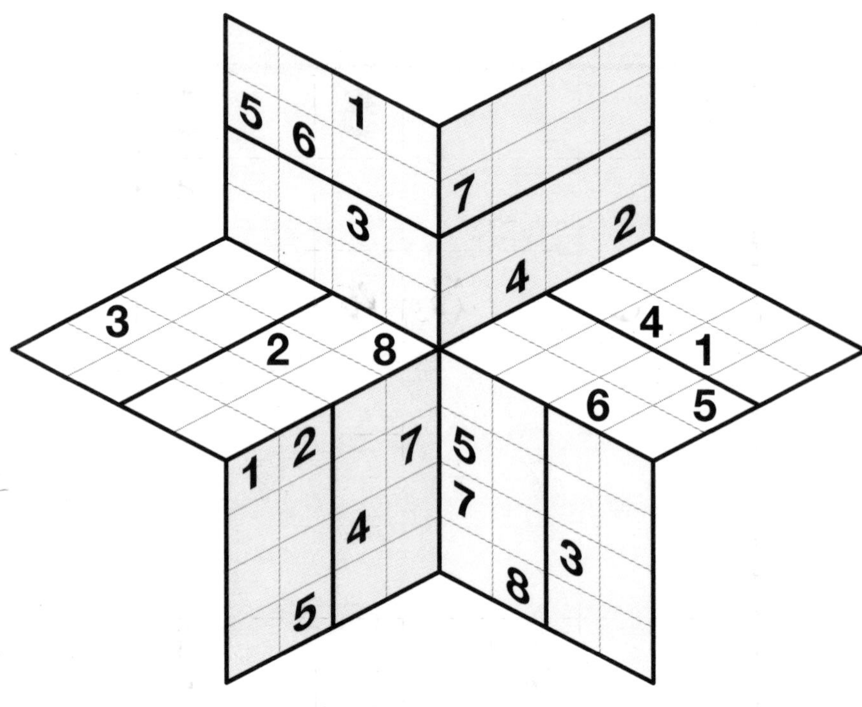

No Repeats

Can you write a number from 1 to 7 in each empty square, so that every row and column of the grid contains each number exactly once?

1				5		2
						6
	5		3	4		
	1				7	
		7	6		3	
2						
5		6				7

Missing Vowels

All of the vowels have been deleted from the following words. Can you restore them by working out what the original words were?

RMFF

WSHRM

RBCS

MSHRM

KNGR

Word Depository

Fit all the listed words into the grid, crossword-style.

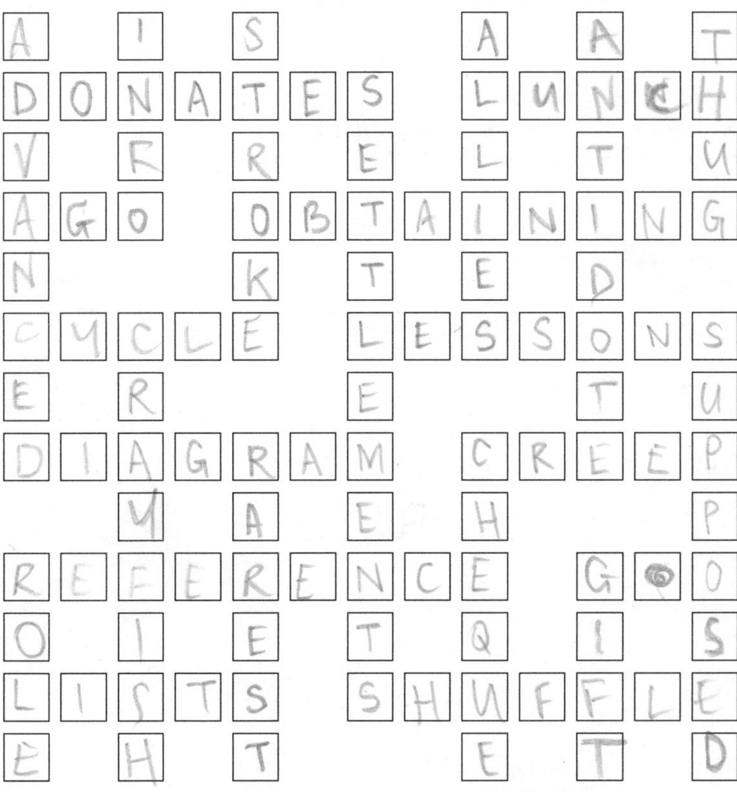

3 Letters
Ago
Goo

4 Letters
Gift
Info
Role
Thug

5 Letters
Creep
Cycle
Lists
Lunch

6 Letters
Allies
Cheque
Rarest
Stroke

7 Letters
Diagram
Donates
Lessons
Shuffle

8 Letters
Advanced
Antidote
Crayfish
Supposed

9 Letters
Obtaining
Reference

11 Letters
Settlements

Memory List

It's a good mindfulness technique to make a list of all the things you need to remember, so you don't worry about forgetting them. But this doesn't mean you should never exercise your memory!

Spend up to a minute remembering the list of gemstones below, then cover it over, wait a few seconds, and then see how many you can write out again in the gaps at the bottom of the page.

Diamond	Ruby	Sapphire
Topaz	Moonstone	Amber
Garnet	Jade	Amethyst
Opal	Agate	Emerald

______________	______________	______________
______________	______________	______________
______________	______________	______________
______________	______________	______________

Mental Maths

Massage your brain with these maths calculations – do as many as you can without using a calculator or making written notes.

12 × 9 =	81	9 × 6 =	54
12 × 16 =	192	84 ÷ 7 =	12
14 + 92 =	106	76 + 19 =	95
26 + 91 =	117	9 × 14 =	126
9 × 5 =	45	182 ÷ 7 =	27
9 × 15 =	135	41 + 9 =	50
13 × 2 =	26	30 - 25 =	5
43 - 29 =	14	11 × 5 =	55
49 - 29 =	20	18 + 18 =	36
8 × 6 =	48	10 - 6 =	4

Arrow Word

All of this crossword's clues are given inside the grid.

Nonsense		Temporary apprentice		Favouritism		Place of education		Substitute
Conceptual		Great expanse of water		Wight or Man, eg				
								Conscious action
Nectar gatherer				Garden hut				
Make money					It's mined for minerals			
Pointing word		Climb onto		Badger burrow	Binary digit			
			Spiritedness		Youngster			
Not drunk						Clangour		Change the colour of
Cause pain to					Completed			
Forbid	Bad hair discovery				Evergreen climbing plant			
				Thigh to lower leg joint				

Every Other Letter

In the following list of musical instruments, every other letter has been removed. Can you restore the missing letters to reveal the full set of instruments?

_A_P_P_S

A_C_R_I_N

_L_C_E_S_I_L

_A_O_H_N_

_E_O_D_R

Letter Circle

How many words of three or more letters can you find in this letter circle? Each word should use the centre letter plus two or more of the other letters, and no letter can be used more than once in a single word. There is one word that uses every letter.

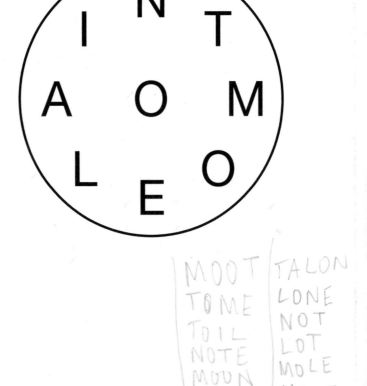

Fancy a challenge? If so, can you find 50 words?

Angular Movement

Colour these squares with two strongly contrasting colours, like a distorted chessboard. Do the shapes now slide, and the lines bend?

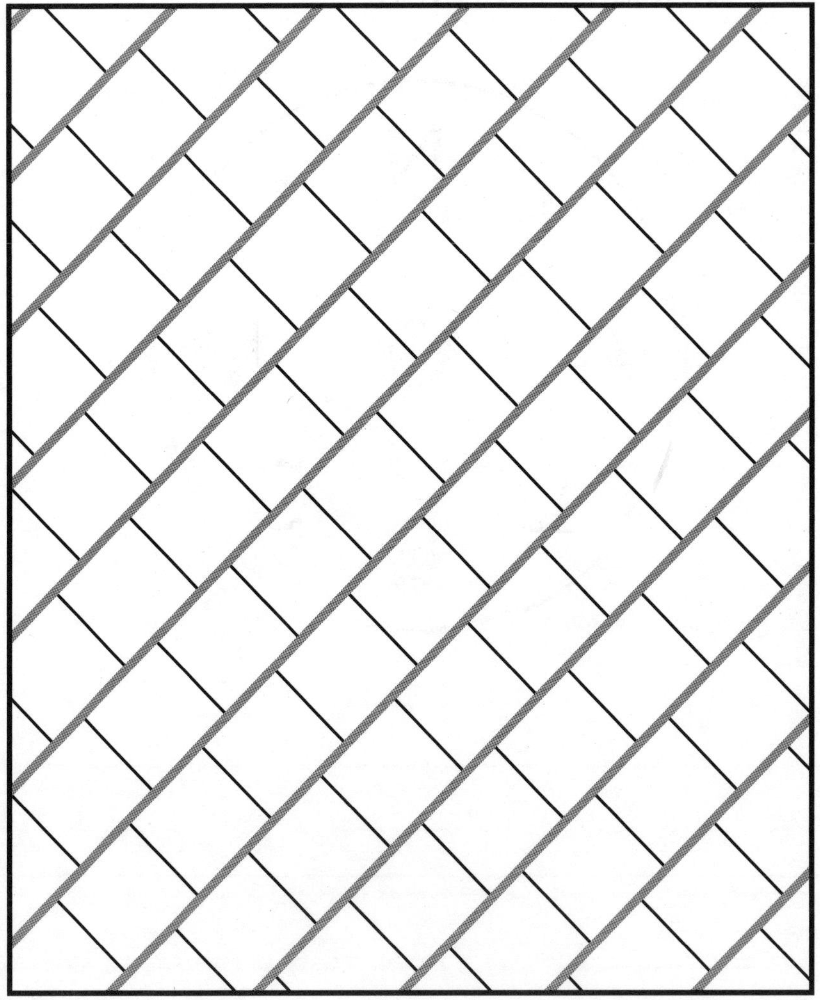

Ordered Recall

First, cover up the bottom of the page (below the dividing line), then spend up to a minute remembering the order of the list of palindromes below, then cover it over, wait a few seconds, and then see if you can recall the order that they were given in. You'll be given the list again.

1. Minim
2. Noon
3. Deed
4. Sagas
5. Madam
6. Deified
7. Tenet
8. Solos
9. Bib
10. Civic
11. Refer
12. Wow
13. Kayak
14. Level
15. Mum

Bib	Civic	Deed	Deified
Kayak	Level	Madam	Minim
Mum	Noon	Refer	Sagas
Solos	Tenet	Wow	

__________	__________	__________
__________	__________	__________
__________	__________	__________
__________	__________	__________
__________	__________	__________

A Circular Route

Can you find your way through this circular maze, travelling from the entrance at the top all the way down to the exit at the bottom?

Minesweeper

Can you work out where the hidden mines are? Some of the empty squares contain mines – mark them in. Clues in some squares show the number of mines in touching squares, including diagonally touching squares. No more than one mine may be placed per square.

2				2	
2		4	3		2
	4				1
	4		4	2	
2				2	
1			2	2	1

Deleted Pairs

Delete one letter from each touching pair of letters to reveal four hidden words, one per row. For example, CD AL TM would lead to C~~D~~ A~~L~~ T~~M~~, revealing CAT.

ET NE ST TA NS

HS EI DC RD AE LN

CT RL EI VR EI AD

HW EO MN ND EO RD SE

Mini Crossword

Solve each of the clues to complete this mini-crossword grid.

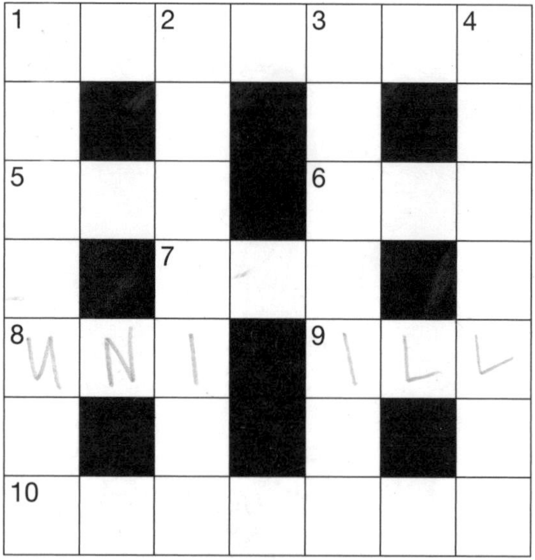

Across

1 Inhabitant (7)
5 Toboggan runner (3)
6 In favour of (3)
7 Remove branches from (3)
8 Place of higher education (3)
9 Diseased (3)
10 Hires (7)

Down

1 Quarrel (7)
2 Hammering (7)
3 Moving suddenly and rapidly (7)
4 Narrow strips of pasta (7)

Word Orbit

By picking one letter from each orbit in turn, working in from the outermost ring to the innermost ring, how many four-letter words can you find?

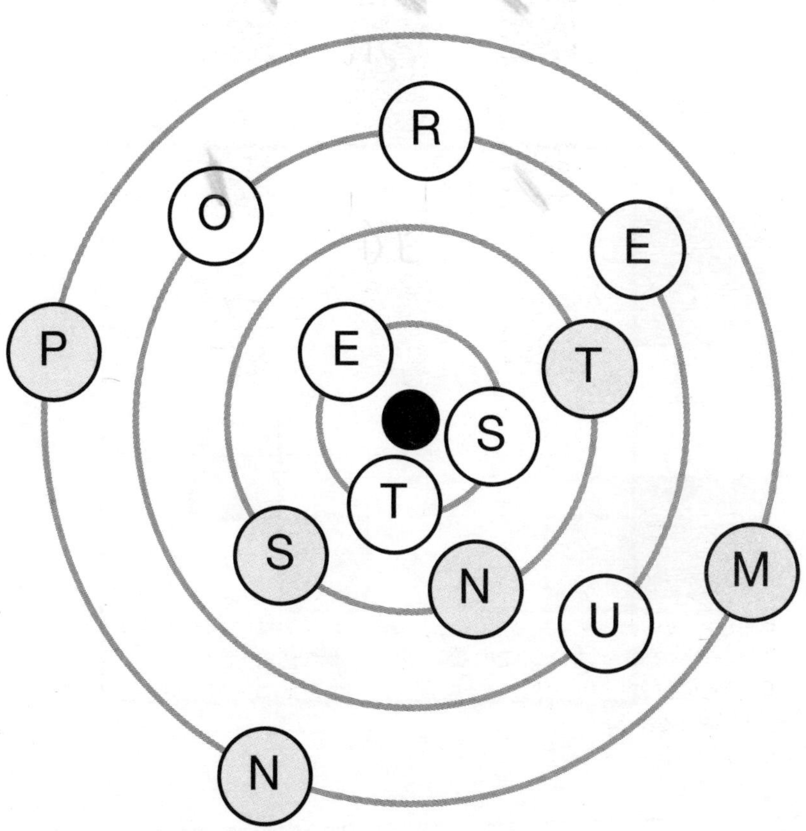

Find the Path

Join some of the dots with horizontal and vertical lines to form a single path. The path should not touch or cross either itself or any of the solid blocks. Numbers outside the grid specify the exact number of dots in their row or column that are visited by the path. The start and end of the path are given to you, and are marked by the solid dots.

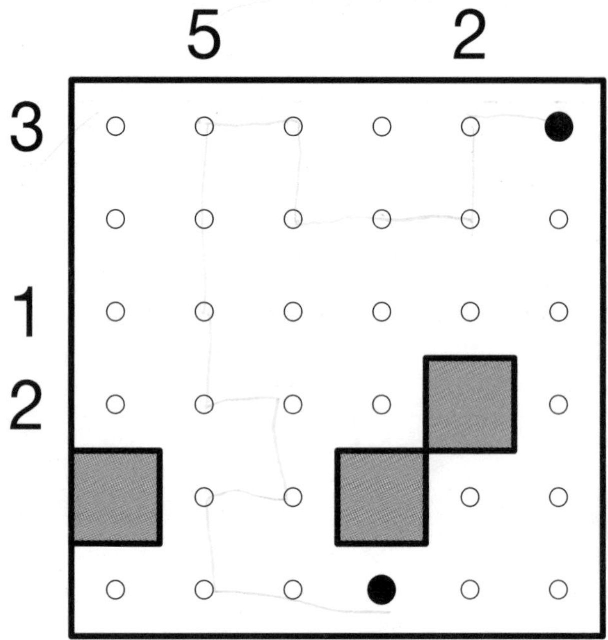

Rhyming Lines

See if you can come up with a rhyming second line for each of these extremely brief poems – the more ridiculous the better!

A cloudy day is time for me,

BOIL THE KETTLE, LETS HAVE SOME TEA

With nature's beauty all around,

I saw a falling leaf float down,

Re-rooming

Each of the following phrases can be rearranged to form the name of a room. Can you solve them all?

RAY BIRL

CARRY-ON VOTES

THE NICK

ME ABSENT

HAM ROBOT

Just for Fun

See if you can come up with an amusing or witty conclusion to each of these partial jokes! There are no correct answers here – the idea is just to provide a bit of creative relaxation.

What do you get if you cross a butterfly and a dragonfly?

____

Did you hear the one about the dog that walked into the pub?

____

Two ducks splash-land on a paddling pool. One duck says to the other:

"_______________________________________"

A Puzzle About Puzzles

Can you find all of the listed puzzles in the grid? They are written forwards or backwards in any direction, including diagonally.

R	M	D	S	S	U	D	O	K	U	R	S	N	G	F
S	U	E	I	I	E	C	A	O	E	G	U	O	U	E
R	E	O	O	O	M	C	R	C	K	M	L	T	I	S
E	G	O	C	A	R	P	T	O	B	A	O	E	N	O
D	L	U	N	E	S	A	L	E	S	S	K	O	A	R
D	H	N	S	I	N	S	R	E	H	S	H	U	E	L
A	G	C	H	G	M	L	S	I	L	R	W	R	R	A
L	W	R	L	S	I	O	K	A	M	O	O	O	O	O
D	S	E	S	N	H	I	D	O	O	S	O	N	R	I
R	S	S	K	D	R	O	W	T	I	F	S	P	M	D
O	E	N	E	A	D	A	R	R	O	W	W	O	R	D
W	Z	O	R	H	C	R	A	E	S	D	R	O	W	G
E	A	W	G	K	B	R	I	D	G	E	S	E	E	O
A	M	A	N	A	G	R	A	M	S	L	R	R	I	S
S	L	I	T	H	E	R	L	I	N	K	L	F	O	D

ANAGRAMS
ARROW WORD
BRIDGES
CROSSWORD
DOMINOES
FITWORD
FUTOSHIKI
KAKURO
MAZE
NUMBER LINK
RECTANGLES
SIMPLE LOOP
SLITHERLINK
SUDOKU
WORD LADDER
WORD SEARCH

Mental Maths

Massage your brain with these maths calculations – do as many as you can without using a calculator or making written notes.

100 ÷ 5 = ☐	74 - 21 = ☐
52 - 24 = ☐	97 + 7 = ☐
15 + 23 = ☐	78 - 15 = ☐
23 + 92 = ☐	8 × 12 = ☐
29 - 23 = ☐	10 + 56 = ☐
8 - 7 = ☐	16 - 12 = ☐
56 + 6 = ☐	6 × 3 = ☐
58 ÷ 2 = ☐	62 - 9 = ☐
92 - 10 = ☐	114 ÷ 2 = ☐
125 ÷ 5 = ☐	41 + 9 = ☐

Word Sliders

How many five-letter words can you spell out using the sliders? One word is spelled out for you already. Each slider can be slid up or down to reveal a single letter.

Simple Loop

Draw a single loop that visits every empty square once each, using just horizontal and vertical lines.

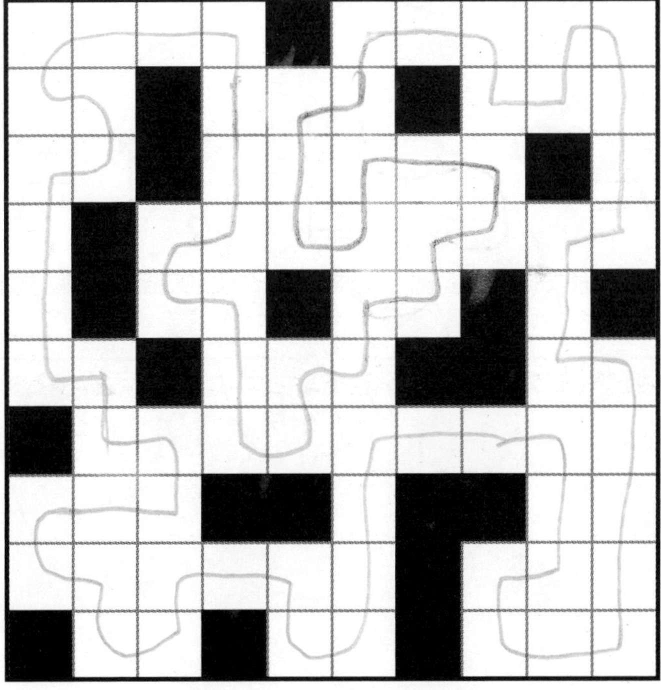

Number Darts

Can you make each of the totals shown below this number dartboard? For each total, choose one number from the inner ring, one number from the middle ring, and one number from the outer ring. The three numbers must add to the given total.

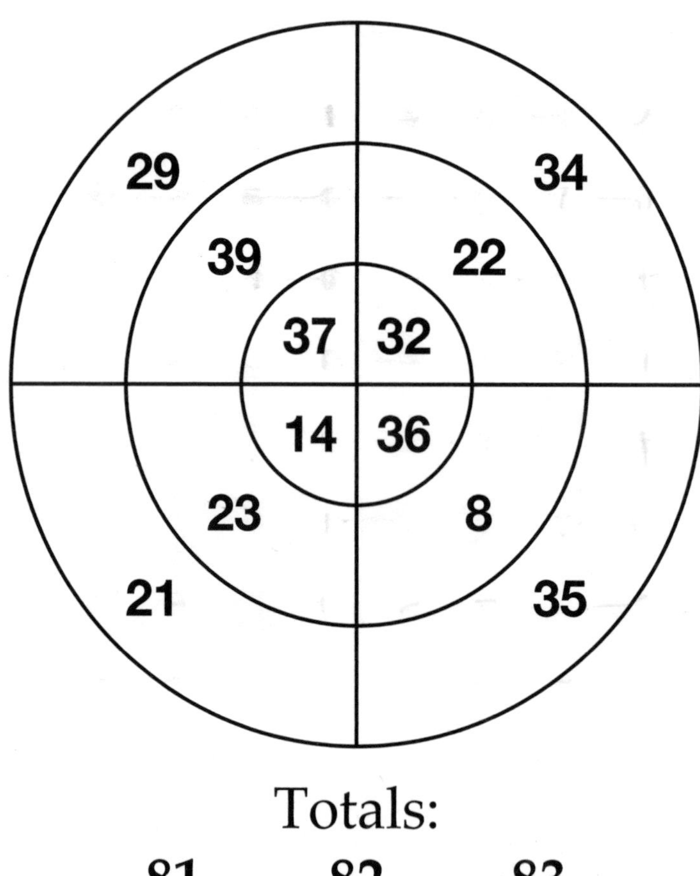

Totals:

81 82 83

Loop the Loop

Join all of the dots using only horizontal or vertical lines to form a single loop. The loop can only visit each dot once, and it can't cross over or touch itself at any point.

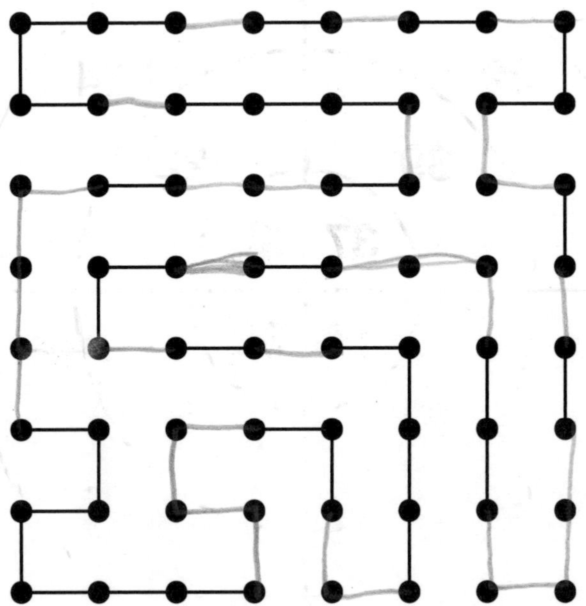

Return of the Word Ladder

Can you transform COME into BACK in just five steps? At each step you should change a single letter to form a new word, but without rearranging the order of any of the letters. For example, you could start by stepping from COME to CONE, and then from CONE to BONE.

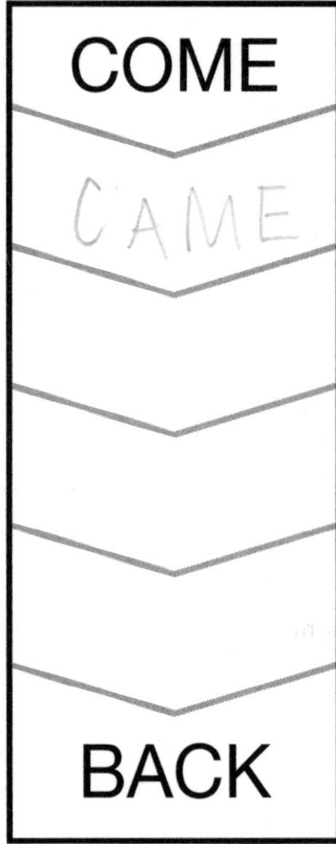

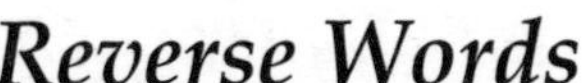

Reverse Words

Can you solve each of the following clues? Each pair of clues reveal the same word, except that the solution to each 'b' clue is the **reverse** of the 'a' clue. For example, if the 'a' solution is DOG then the 'b' solution will be GOD, and vice versa.

Puzzle 1
a. Certain fortified wines
b. Temper tantrum, informally

Puzzle 2
a. Animal pads
b. Exchange

Puzzle 3
a. Ball-striking game
b. Try to sell, informally

Puzzle 4
a. Send money in payment
b. Duration recorder

Classic Maze

Can you find your way through this square maze, travelling from the entrance at the top all the way down to the exit at the bottom?

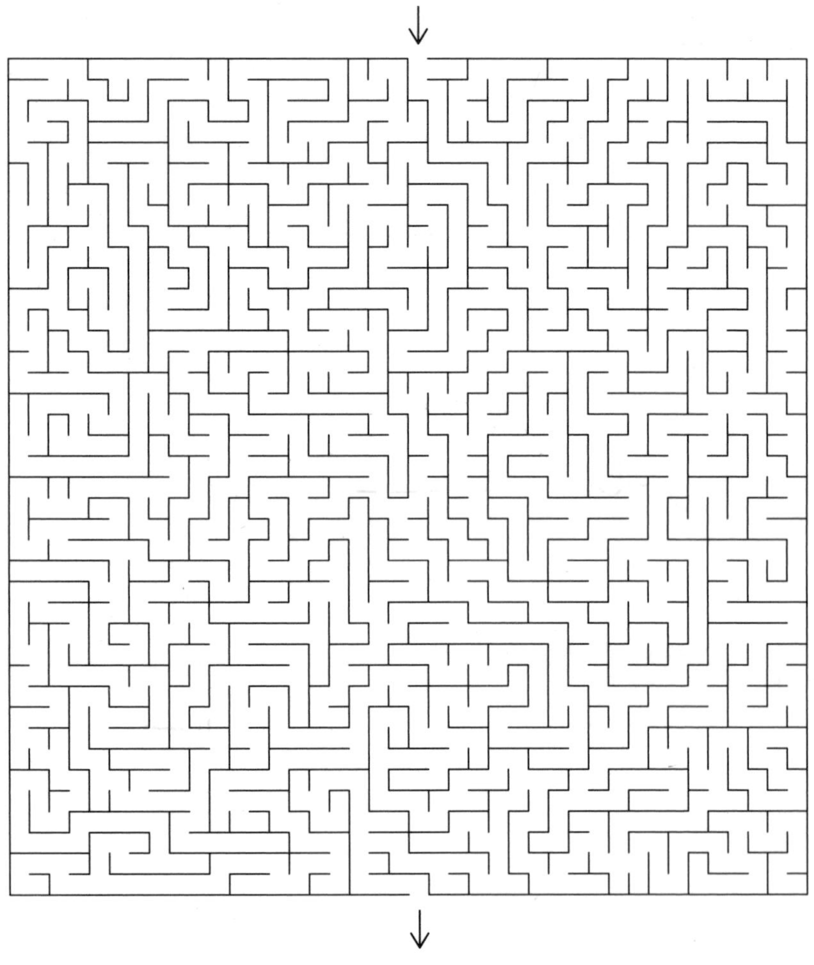

Link Words

Find a common English word to place in each gap, so that both when attached to the end of the first word and when attached to the start of the second word you end up with two more English words. For example, **birth _ _ _ break** could be solved using **day**, making **birthday** and **daybreak**.

over _ _ _ _ _ less

sign _ _ _ _ age

corn _ _ _ _ _ winner

Word Paths

How many words of three or more letters can you find in this square? Find words by moving horizontally or vertically (but not diagonally) from letter to touching letter, and without revisiting a square in a single word. There is also one word that uses every letter.

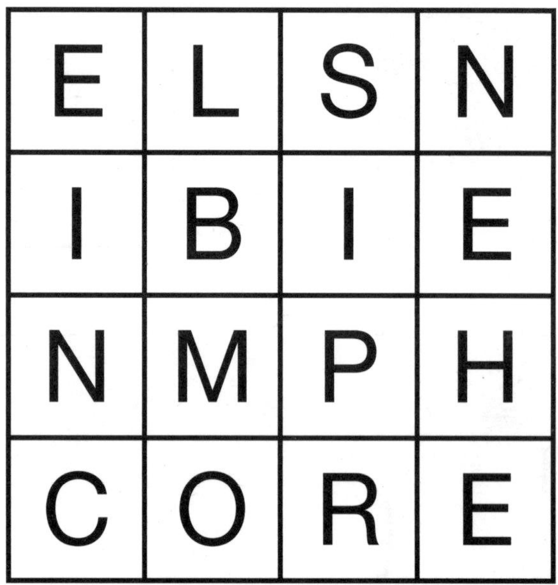

E	L	S	N
I	B	I	E
N	M	P	H
C	O	R	E

Fancy a challenge? If so, can you find 15 words?

Grid Memory

Look at the pattern in the grid at the top-left of the page, then cover it over and see if you can accurately reproduce it in the empty grid at the top-right of the page. Then repeat with each of the other two grids.

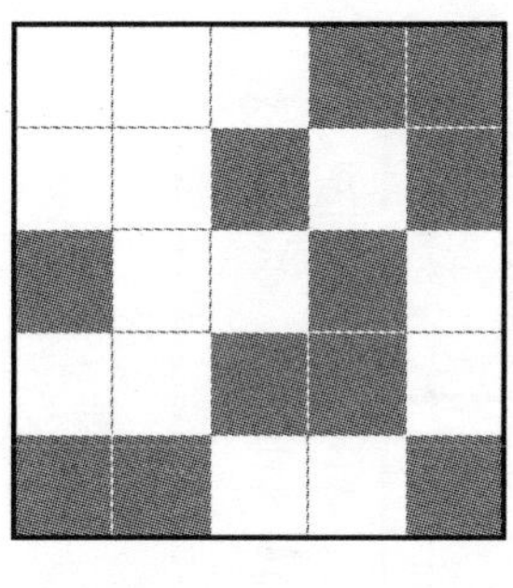

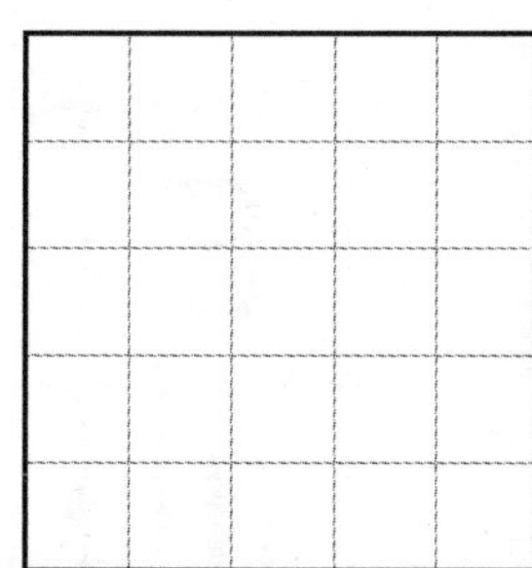

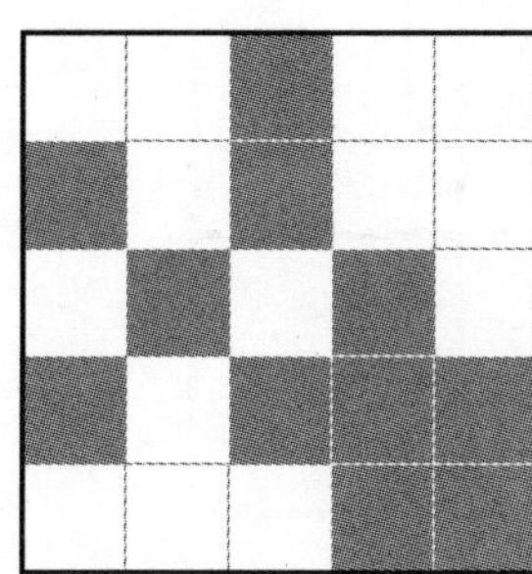

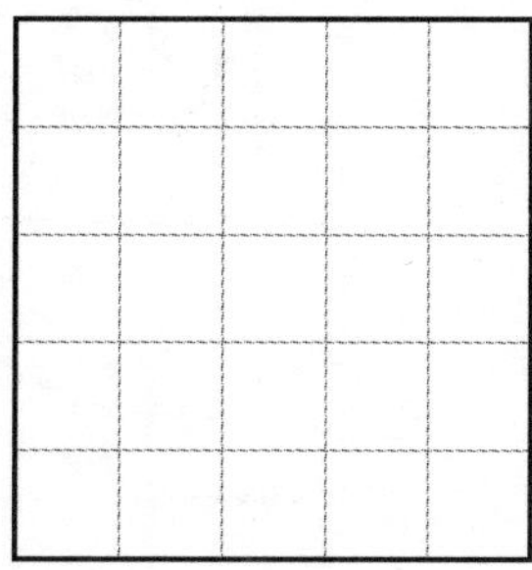

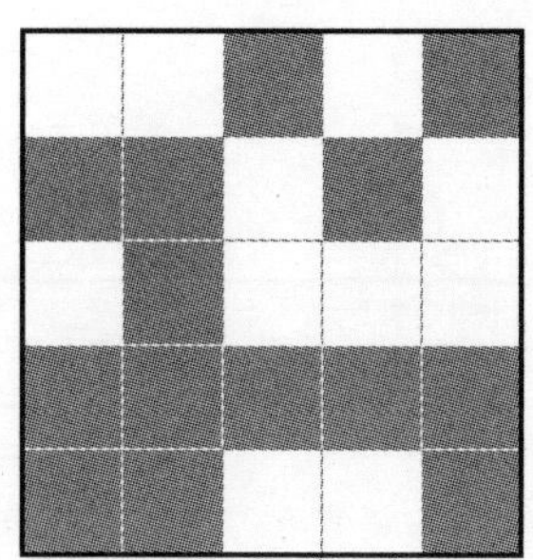

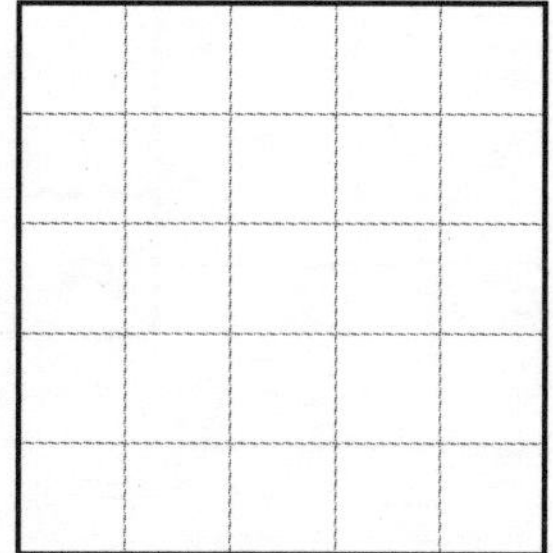

Jigsaw Letters

To solve these puzzles, place a letter from A to E in each empty square so that every row, column and bold-lined jigsaw shape contains each letter exactly once.

Puzzle 1

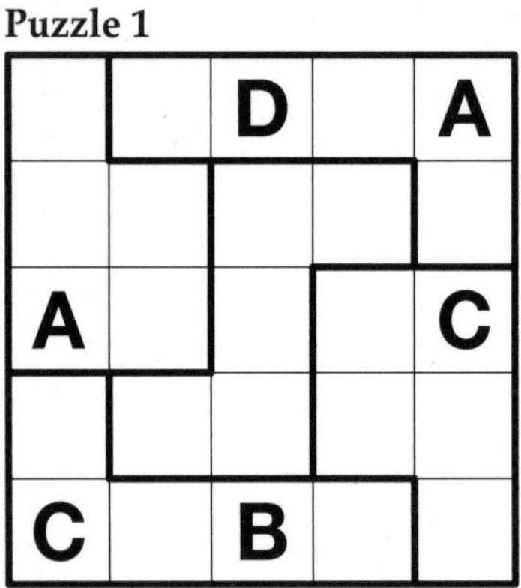

Puzzle 2

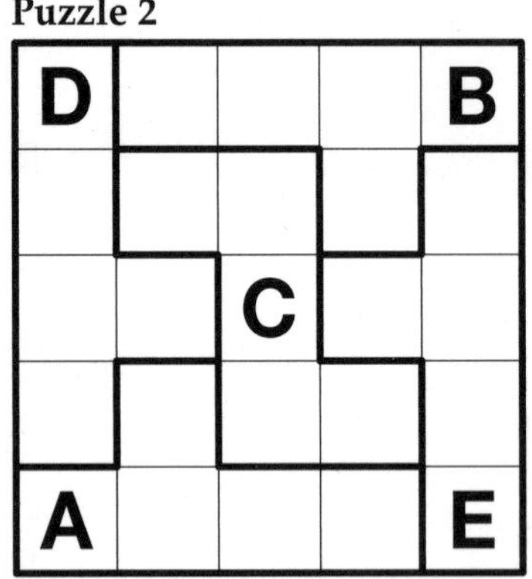

Anagram Pairs

Draw lines to join each word in the left-hand column to a word in the right-hand column, where the two words are anagrams of one another. For example, you could join MELONS to LEMONS.

Phased	Presto
Pierce	Recipe
Player	Replay
Poster	Sanded
Priest	Shaped
Primes	Simper
Pseudo	Singer
Reigns	Siring
Resets	Sister
Resist	Souped
Rising	Steers
Rivets	Stripe
Rushes	Strive
Sadden	Theses
Sheets	Ushers

Missing Symbols

Give your mind a workout by writing the missing mathematical sign into each of these equations: +, −, × or ÷.

63	☐	15 = 48		14	☐	29 = 43
31	☐	7 = 24		2	☐	9 = 18
56	☐	1 = 55		57	☐	15 = 72
14	☐	5 = 19		13	☐	5 = 8
54	☐	6 = 9		8	☐	10 = 80
69	☐	17 = 86		15	☐	9 = 24
20	☐	4 = 5		51	☐	6 = 57
6	☐	4 = 24		28	☐	18 = 46
31	☐	11 = 42		144	☐	12 = 12
18	☐	2 = 20		74	☐	14 = 88

Mini Crossword

Solve each of the clues to complete this mini-crossword grid.

Across
1 Male swine (4)
4 A billion years (3)
6 Trails (7)
7 A score of zero (3)
8 Mythical hairy snow-monster (4)

Down
2 Parentless child (6)
3 Without hesitation (7)
5 Freshest (6)

Rectangles and Squares

Draw along some of the dashed lines to divide the grid into a set of rectangles and squares, so that every rectangle or square contains exactly one number. That number must always be equal to the number of grid squares within the rectangle or square.

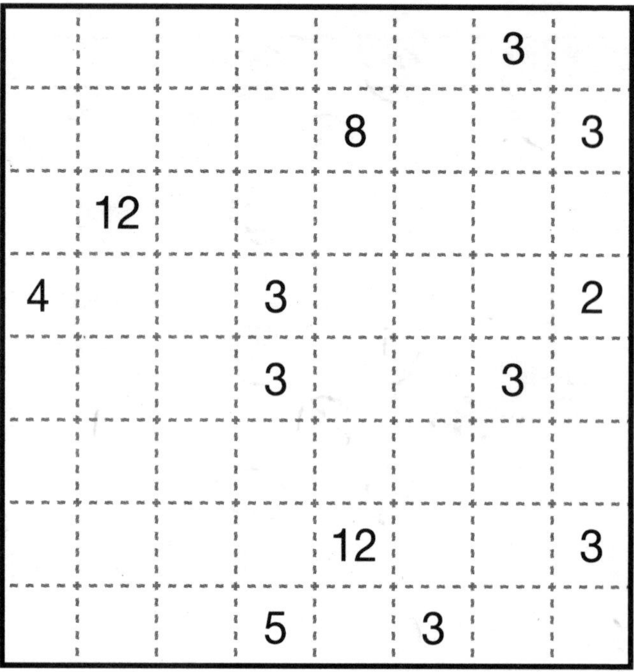

						3	
				8			3
	12						
4			3				2
			3			3	
				12			3
			5		3		

Bridges

Draw horizontal and vertical lines to represent bridges joining these numbered islands. Bridges can't cross over either each other or another island, and you must build the bridges in such a way that you could travel from one island to any other using just the bridges. There can be no more than one bridge between any given pair of islands, and each island must have the given number of bridges connected to it.

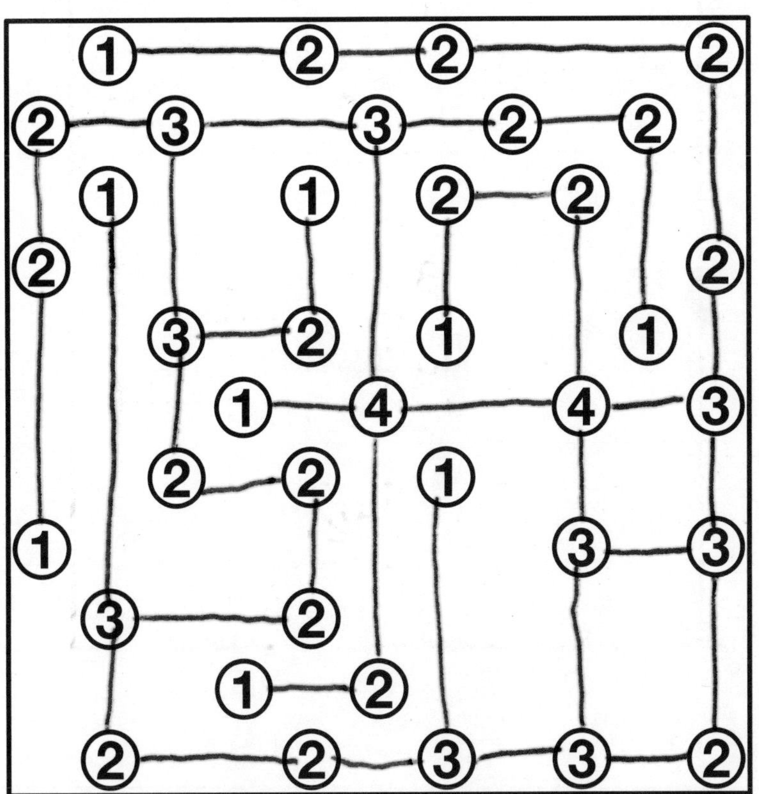

Words Away

Fit all the listed words into the grid, crossword-style.

3 Letters
Egg
Phi

4 Letters
Song
Took

5 Letters
Among
Optic
Spasm
Usage

6 Letters
Invade
Nested
Pounds
Season
Techno
Voodoo

7 Letters
Scatter
Unclear

8 Letters
Crossing
Debugged

9 Letters
Fictional
Lecturing
Transport

13 Letters
International
Psychological

Start and End

For each of these puzzles, add the same letter to both the start and end of the given fragment to form a normal English word. For example, add S to _TART_ to form STARTS.

WILI

_HI_

EER

RAI

LERI

ALVO

_LA_

Number Link

Draw a series of separate paths, each connecting a pair of identical numbers. Paths only travel horizontally or vertically, and they don't cross or touch at any point. No more than one path can enter any grid square.

1					2				
		3	1					4	5
		6						7	
							8	4	
	6				9				
				10					
		5							
			9						
3			10				8		
2									7

Time Totals

Exercise your mind with these time calculations. Just add the two times, or subtract the second time from the first as appropriate.

19:55 + 01:40 = [:]

14:00 + 05:55 = [:]

13:35 - 08:45 = [:]

18:05 + 04:55 = [:]

06:45 + 10:45 = [:]

11:50 + 05:35 = [:]

05:45 - 04:15 = [:]

18:45 - 13:45 = [:]

04:15 + 05:00 = [:]

11:05 + 06:45 = [:]

Touchy Letters

Place one letter from A to F into every empty box, so that each row and column contains all six different letters. Also, identical letters can't be in touching boxes – not even diagonally.

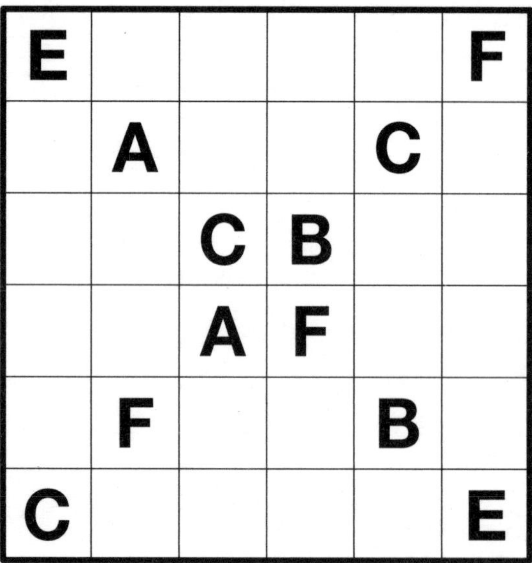

E					F
	A			C	
		C	B		
		A	F		
	F			B	
C					E

Futoshiki

Place 1 to 5 once each in every row and column, while obeying the greater-than signs – if there is a sign between two squares, then the arrow always points at the smaller of the two numbers.

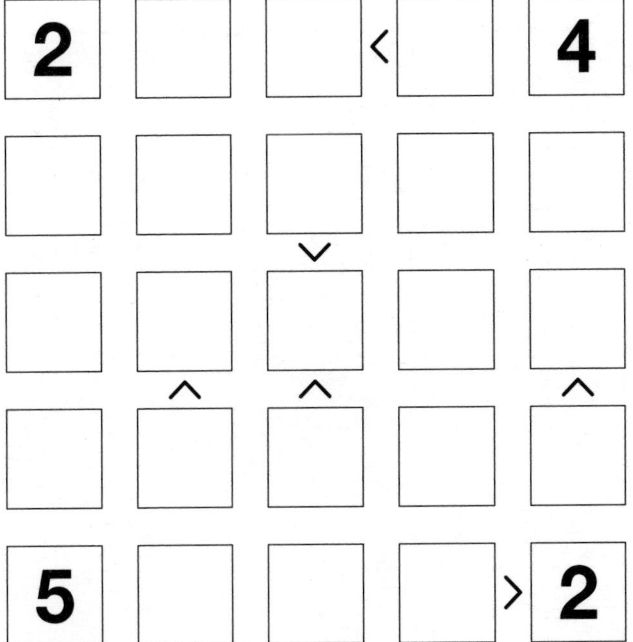

Spot the Changes

First, cover up the bottom of the page (below the dividing line), then spend up to a minute remembering the list of sports below, then cover it over, wait a few seconds, and then see if you can spot which ones have been replaced on the copy of the list at the bottom of the page.

Curling
Volleyball
Lacrosse
Cycling
Football

Snooker
Golf
Netball
Basketball
Skating

Tennis
Bowling
Rugby
Archery
Windsurfing

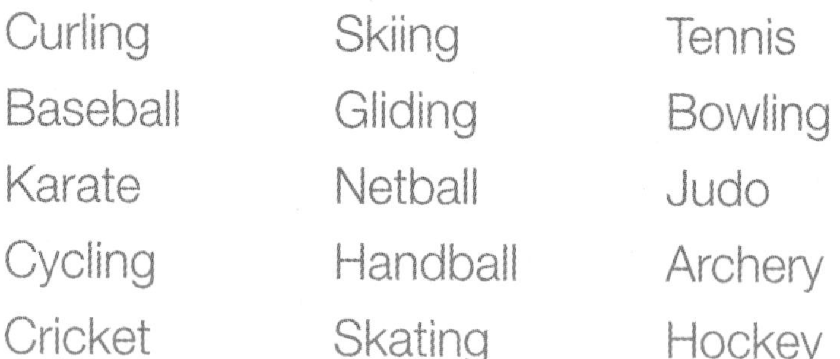

Curling
Baseball
Karate
Cycling
Cricket

Skiing
Gliding
Netball
Handball
Skating

Tennis
Bowling
Judo
Archery
Hockey

Hourglass Maze

Can you find your way through this hourglass-shaped maze, travelling from the entrance at the top all the way down to the exit at the bottom?

Brain Chains

Can you solve each of the three brain chains completely in your head, without making any written notes? Start with the bold number at the top, and then apply each maths operation in turn. Write your final result in at the bottom.

5

+12

-4

+18

-15

+50%

RESULT

40

×4

÷10

+72

×1/2

-25%

RESULT

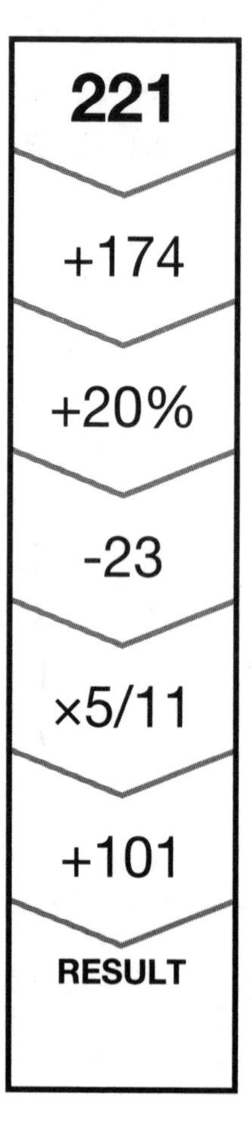

It's a Dog's Life

Can you find all of the listed breeds of dog in the grid? They are written forwards or backwards in any direction, including diagonally.

E	L	P	R	R	R	R	L	L	P	O	R	L	E	P
L	S	P	L	E	E	A	R	K	I	E	E	R	R	O
N	G	H	I	L	V	A	A	G	I	L	I	I	O	A
M	R	Z	G	N	P	E	R	R	L	P	R	S	D	Z
K	K	A	Z	O	S	D	I	E	U	D	R	S	A	E
P	E	E	O	T	C	C	S	R	N	N	E	L	R	L
B	N	D	L	O	I	S	H	U	T	K	T	I	B	N
P	L	H	L	P	U	P	H	E	L	E	D	K	A	I
E	A	L	U	R	I	S	S	E	R	H	R	O	L	T
N	I	P	K	S	H	E	K	E	P	E	L	E	A	N
E	I	C	O	C	K	E	R	S	P	A	N	I	E	L
L	A	A	A	L	L	Y	E	A	I	T	O	O	R	O
J	E	D	A	D	A	L	M	A	T	I	A	N	Z	E
T	D	A	S	P	S	H	E	E	P	D	O	G	E	H
A	R	E	Z	U	A	N	H	C	S	I	E	O	D	E

BEAGLE
COCKER SPANIEL
COLLIE
DACHSHUND
DALMATIAN
HUSKY
JACK RUSSELL
KELPIE
LABRADOR
PINSCHER
POODLE
RETRIEVER
SCHNAUZER
SHEEPDOG
SPITZ
TERRIER

Domino Fit

Draw solid lines to divide the grid into a full set of standard dominoes, with exactly one of each domino. A '0' represents a blank on a traditional domino. Use the check-off chart to help you keep track of which dominoes you've placed.

1	0	2	2	3	2	4	3
0	4	5	6	3	5	5	1
0	0	6	4	4	2	4	0
5	2	6	0	4	2	3	3
0	2	4	6	2	6	1	1
5	1	3	5	5	5	1	1
1	6	6	3	3	0	4	6

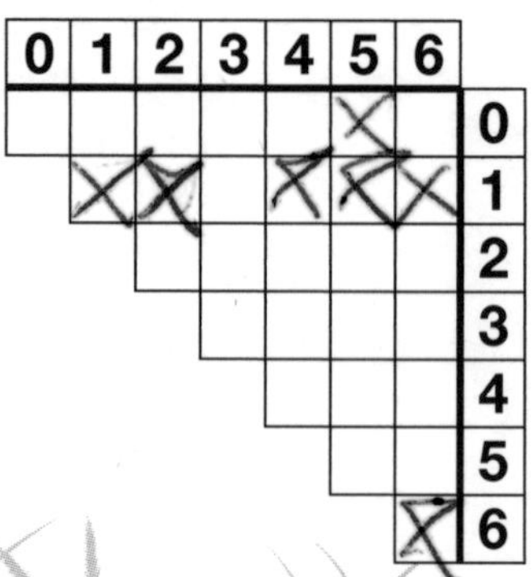

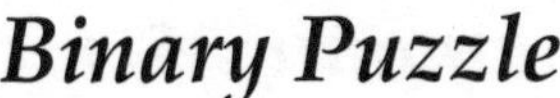

Binary Puzzle

Place a 0 or 1 in every empty square so that each row and column contains four '0's and four '1's. No more than two '0's or two '1's can appear consecutively in any row or column.

<table>
<tr><td></td><td>0</td><td></td><td>0</td><td></td><td>1</td><td>0</td><td>1</td></tr>
<tr><td></td><td></td><td>1</td><td></td><td></td><td></td><td>1</td><td></td></tr>
<tr><td>1</td><td>1</td><td></td><td>1</td><td></td><td></td><td></td><td></td></tr>
<tr><td></td><td></td><td></td><td>1</td><td></td><td></td><td>0</td><td></td></tr>
<tr><td></td><td>1</td><td></td><td></td><td>0</td><td></td><td></td><td></td></tr>
<tr><td></td><td></td><td></td><td></td><td>1</td><td></td><td>1</td><td>1</td></tr>
<tr><td></td><td>1</td><td></td><td></td><td></td><td>1</td><td></td><td></td></tr>
<tr><td>1</td><td>1</td><td>0</td><td></td><td>0</td><td></td><td>1</td><td></td></tr>
</table>

Mnemonic Memory

Using an acronym as a memory aid can really help with remembering a list of items. See if you can use the food acronyms on this page, in the first letter of each column, to help you remember each of the words. Use the lines at the bottom of the page to see how you get on.

Clean	Only	Solid
Real	Novel	Water
Everyday	Individual	Earth
Success	Original	Drowsy
Suits	Nouns	Event

Arrow Word

All of this crossword's clues are given inside the grid.

Japanese feudal warrior		Towered temple		Sand bank		Ahead of time		Bring into action
Haze		Lyric poem		Help in crime				
				'That's right'				Take advantage of
Japanese noodles					Winter ailment			
Opposite of green?				Murmurs softly				
Be into, colloquially		Chewy sweet?		Extra pay	Barley-like grass			
			Casual word of parting				Proposal	Hopping amphibian
Lady	Female reproductive cells		Number of years old		Best-seller			
					Commotion			
Earnings		Conakry is its capital						
					Male role model?			

Number Pyramid

Write a number in every empty block so that each block is equal to the sum of the two blocks directly beneath it.

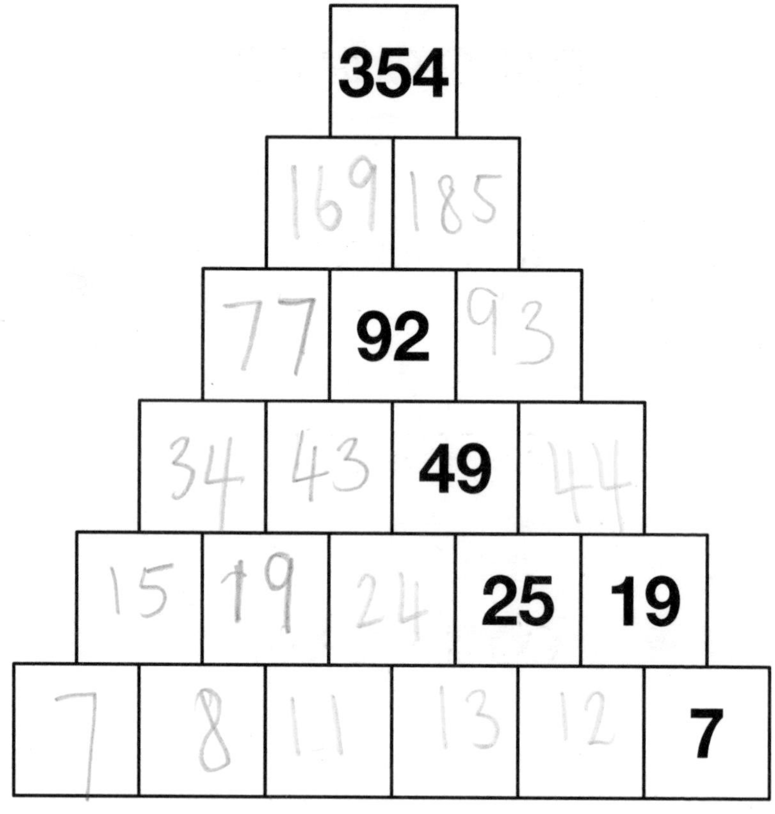

Coffee Time

Each of the following phrases can be rearranged to form the name of a type of coffee. Can you solve them all?

PIANO CUP CC

CAPPUCCINO

AM CHAOTIC

MACCHIATO

SEERS SOP

ESPRESSO

CORE MANIA

AMERICANO

TRIFLE

FILTER

No Repeats

Can you write a number from 1 to 7 in each empty square, so that every row and column of the grid contains each number exactly once?

7		5		1		3
	2		5		3	
1						5
	5				4	
4						6
	4		1		6	
3		7		6		4

Counting Cubes

How many individual cubes have been used to build the structure below? You should assume that all 'hidden' cubes are present, and that it started off as a perfect 5×4×4 arrangement of cubes (as shown to the right) before any cubes were removed. There are no floating cubes.

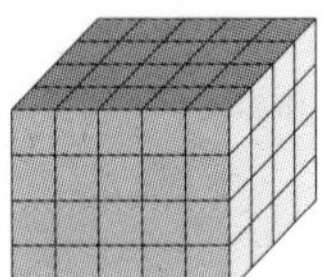

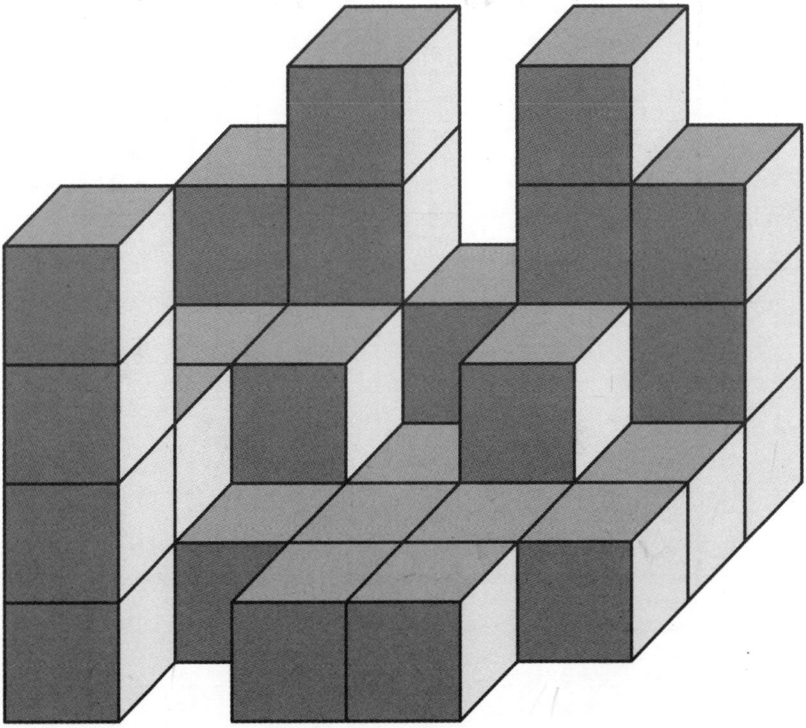

Bridge Maze

Can you find your way through this maze, travelling from the entrance at the top all the way down to the exit at the bottom? The maze contains a number of bridges, which allow you to pass either over or under a path – but not to move between crossing paths.

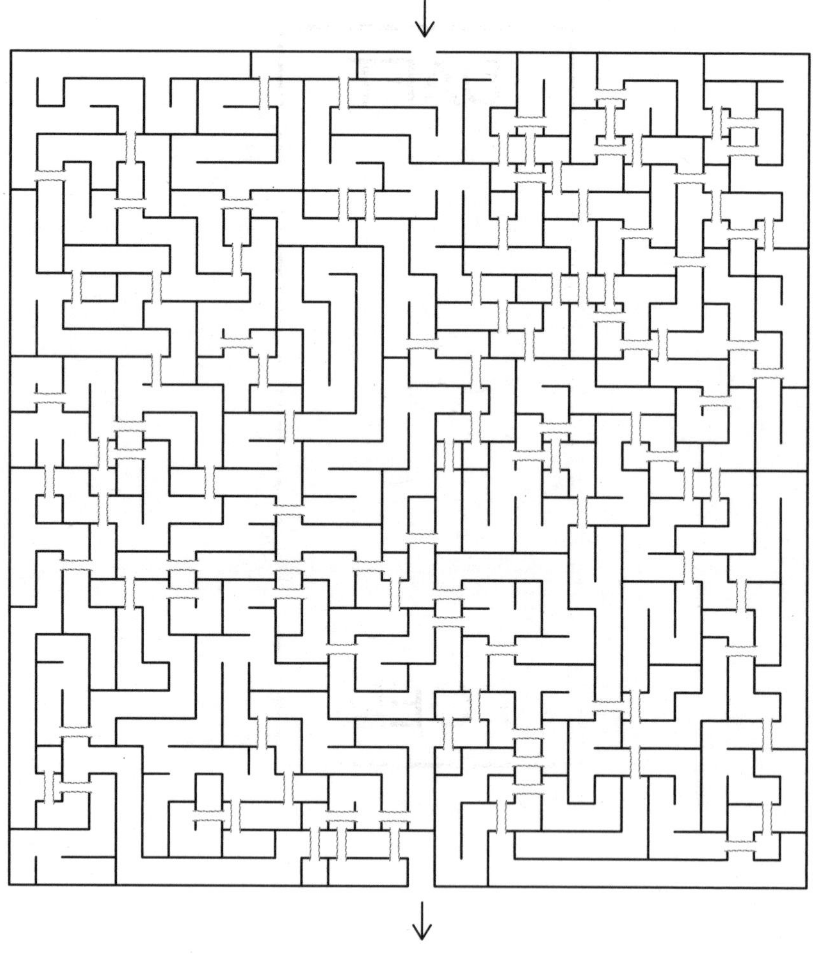

Silly Sonnet

Can you transform DAFT into POEM in just five steps? At each step you should change a single letter to form a new word, but without rearranging the order of any of the letters. For example, you could start by stepping from DAFT to DART, and then from DART to DARN.

At Ease

Rearrange each set of boxes to spell out a series of words that each mean 'relaxed'.

Puzzle 1

BLE	MF	CO	TA	OR

Puzzle 2

RR	D	HU	IE	UN

Puzzle 3

Y	UR	LE	EL	IS

Puzzle 4

EF	E	AR	C	RE

A Circular Route

Can you find your way through this circular maze, travelling from the entrance at the top all the way down to the exit at the bottom?

Calming Drinks

Can you transform LOVE into TEAS in just five steps? At each step you should change a single letter to form a new word, but without rearranging the order of any of the letters. For example, you could start by stepping from LOVE to DOVE, and then from DOVE to DIVE.

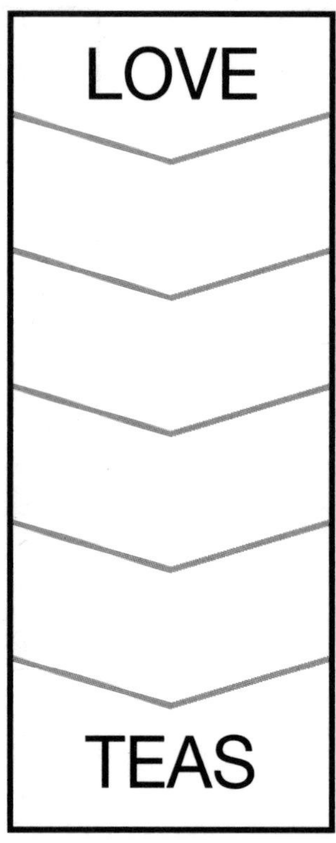

Simple Sudoku

See how quickly you can complete these easy puzzles – just place the digits from 1 to 4 into every row, column and 2×2 box for each puzzle.

Puzzle 1

		2	4
2	1		

Puzzle 2

	2		
		3	
	3		
		4	

Puzzle 3

2	1	4	
	4	1	2

Puzzle 4

			3
	2		
		4	
1			

Some Rearrangement Required

Each of the following phrases can be rearranged to form the name of a colour. Can you solve them all?

RE PULP

QUARE MANIA

COOL CHEAT

GO ANIMAL

NEVER LAD

Bridges

Draw horizontal and vertical lines to represent bridges joining these numbered islands. Bridges can't cross over either each other or another island, and you must build the bridges in such a way that you could travel from one island to any other using just the bridges. There can be no more than one bridge between any given pair of islands, and each island must have the given number of bridges connected to it.

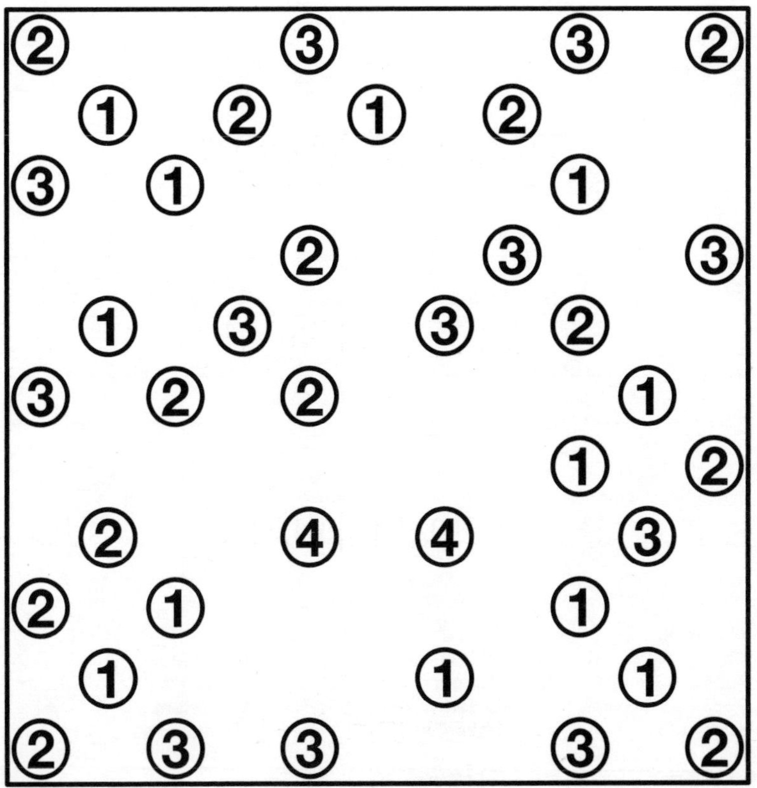

Placing Words

Fit all the listed words into the grid, crossword-style.

4 Letters
Rile
Rubs
Skip
Vamp

5 Letters
Angle
Moody

6 Letters
Advice
Bonsai
Cicada
Ignore
Online
Robots
Sailed
Salami

7 Letters
Parking
Reality

8 Letters
Assemble
Flambeau
Location
Thoracic

11 Letters
Constituted
Initialized

Missing Details

Using your imagination, can you use a pen or pencil to convert these rectangles into pictures of three different **window views**? For example, one could be to distant hills, and another could be to a car just outside.

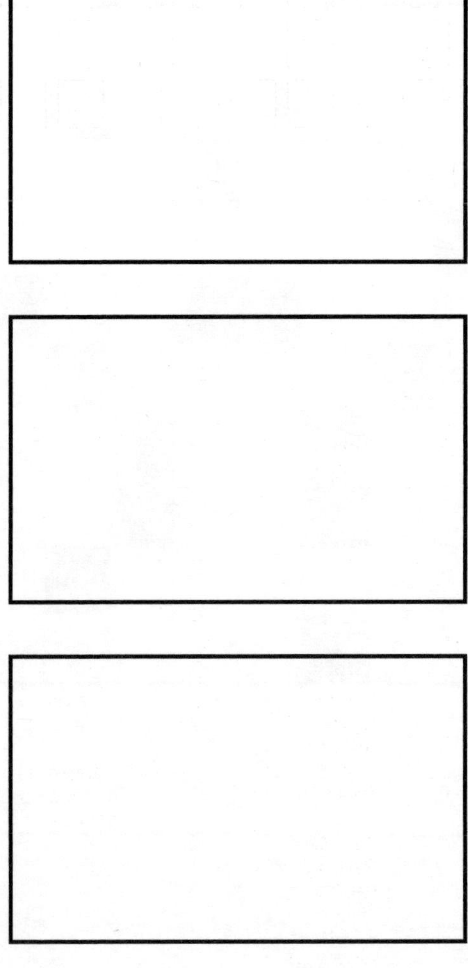

Simple Loop

Draw a single loop that visits every empty square once each, using just horizontal and vertical lines.

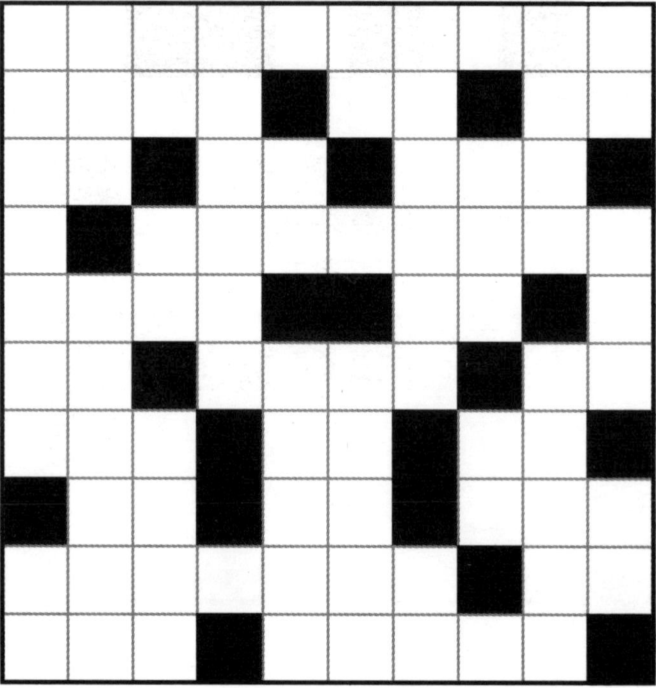

Mini Crossword

Solve each of the clues to complete this mini-crossword grid.

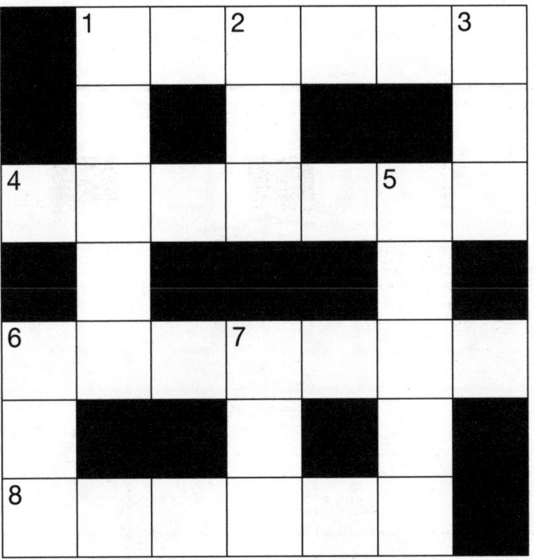

Across

1 Elastic material (6)
4 Set apart (7)
6 Energetic (7)
8 Go aboard (6)

Down

1 Dangerous (5)
2 Audio intensity unit (3)
3 Bewail (3)
5 Prank (5)
6 Female deer (3)
7 Norwegian pop band (1-2)

Word Paths

How many words of three or more letters can you find in this square? Find words by moving horizontally or vertically (but not diagonally) from letter to touching letter, and without revisiting a square in a single word. There is also one word that uses every letter.

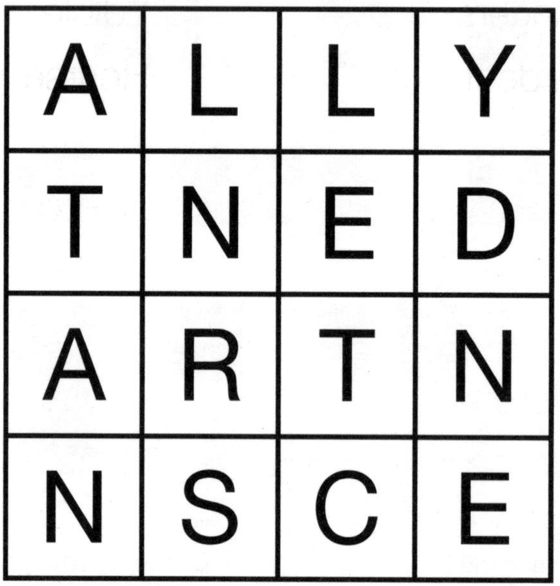

A	L	L	Y
T	N	E	D
A	R	T	N
N	S	C	E

Fancy a challenge? If so, can you find 30 words?

Anagram Pairs

Draw lines to join each word in the left-hand column to a word in the right-hand column, where the two words are anagrams of one another. For example, you could join MELONS to LEMONS.

Angers	Edible
Ardent	Hoarse
Armpit	Impart
Ashore	Nailed
Aspire	Obsess
Assent	Ported
Belied	Praise
Bosses	Ranges
Caress	Ranted
Cedars	Sacred
Creams	Sanest
Decals	Scaled
Decors	Scares
Denial	Scored
Deport	Scream

Reverse Words

Can you solve each of the following clues? Each pair of clues reveal the same word, except that the solution to each 'b' clue is the **reverse** of the 'a' clue. For example, if the 'a' solution is DOG then the 'b' solution will be GOD, and vice versa.

Puzzle 1
a. Temperament
b. Ultimate fate

Puzzle 2
a. Steals
b. Backless chair

Puzzle 3
a. Someone who refuses to accept something
b. What a former king or queen has done

Puzzle 4
a. Fiend
b. Existed

Loop the Loop

Join all of the dots using only horizontal or vertical lines to form a single loop. The loop can only visit each dot once, and it can't cross over or touch itself at any point.

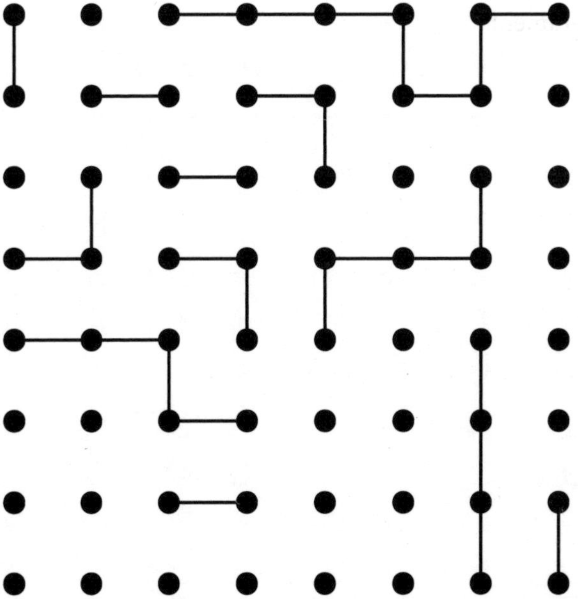

A Shapely Puzzle

Can you find all of the listed shapes in the grid? They are written forwards or backwards in any direction, including diagonally.

```
O X D N O M A I D E S R S E A
N I C D E A E D L G Q I U S R
M R R O H S H S T O U P B P E
A N A M N L C T G P A R M I E
R C E T G O L O R H R L O L H
G E E C S P G E N I E R H L O
O L N A N E Y A I E A L R E N
L T D P E I L R X T L N S O T
E N L L E S N G A E L R G R A
L C A L R N P E N M H A I L T
L A V U G R T H L A I A O D E
A N O O H Y S A E C T D T L O
R O M T T R C Q G R R C C L N
A S O C T A G O N O E I E A R
P D P N A L R E A S N O C R L
```

CIRCLE
CONE
DIAMOND
ELLIPSE
HEXAGON
OCTAGON
OVAL
PARALLELOGRAM
PENTAGON
PYRAMID
RECTANGLE
RHOMBUS
SPHERE
SQUARE
STAR
TRIANGLE

Memory List

It's a good mindfulness technique to make a list of all the things you need to remember, so you don't worry about forgetting them. But this doesn't mean you should never exercise your memory!

Spend up to a minute remembering the list of burger toppings below, then cover it over, wait a few seconds, and then see how many you can write out again in the gaps at the bottom of the page.

Mustard	Avocado	Ketchup
Fried egg	Cheese	Lettuce
Onions	Mayonnaise	Mushrooms
Pickle	Pepper	Bacon

______________	______________	______________
______________	______________	______________
______________	______________	______________
______________	______________	______________

Number Pyramid

Write a number in every empty block so that each block is equal to the sum of the two blocks directly beneath it.

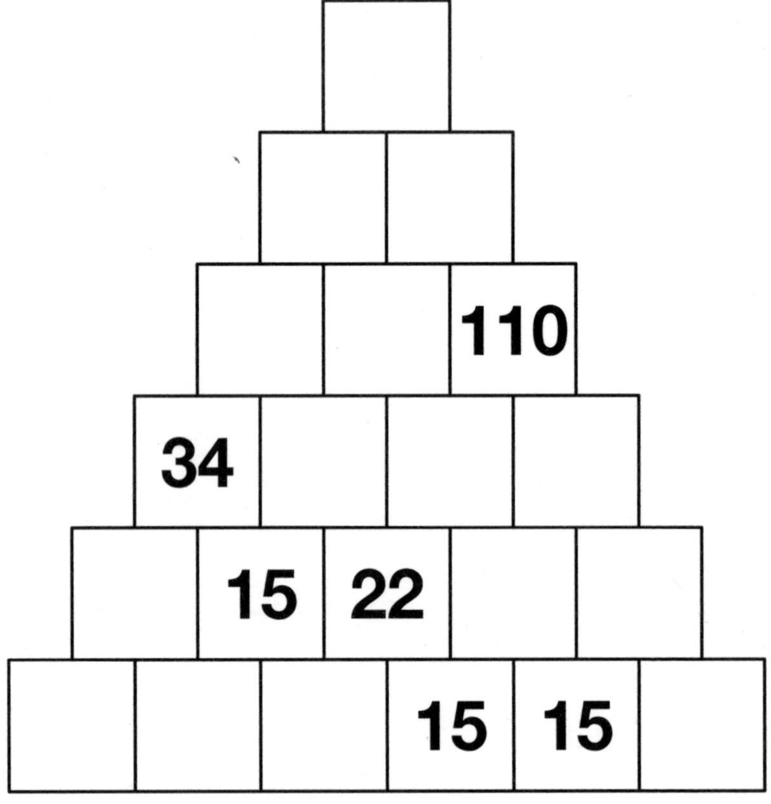

Link Words

Find a common English word to place in each gap, so that both when attached to the end of the first word and when attached to the start of the second word you end up with two more English words. For example, **birth** _ _ _ **break** could be solved using **day**, making **birthday** and **daybreak**.

east _ _ _ _ robe

cat _ _ _ _ out

every _ _ _ _ _ _ upon

Just for Fun

See if you can come up with an amusing or witty conclusion to each of these partial jokes! There are no correct answers here – the idea is just to provide a bit of creative relaxation.

Why did the penguin cross the road?

____

What happened when the three-legged cat took the bus to the park?

____

What's the difference between a stream of drivers and a dream of strivers?

____

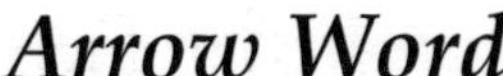

Arrow Word

All of this crossword's clues are given inside the grid.

University awards		Advises against		Count up		Inform		Prefix meaning 'relating to life'
Ova		Pop musician, Lady ___		Metre or kilogram				
				Cow sound				The whole lot
Framework for storing things					Band's live event		Odd; peculiar	
Id counterpart				Young woman				
Gorgeous		Eye up		Fitness club				Mid-month day
Proposed	'Stick your ___ in', to interfere				Clarets, eg	Besmear	Cloned animal, Dolly	
Forces	Fronted				Astonish			

Brain Chains

Can you solve each of the three brain chains completely in your head, without making any written notes? Start with the bold number at the top, and then apply each maths operation in turn. Write your final result in at the bottom.

9

√

×2

+25

-8

+21

RESULT

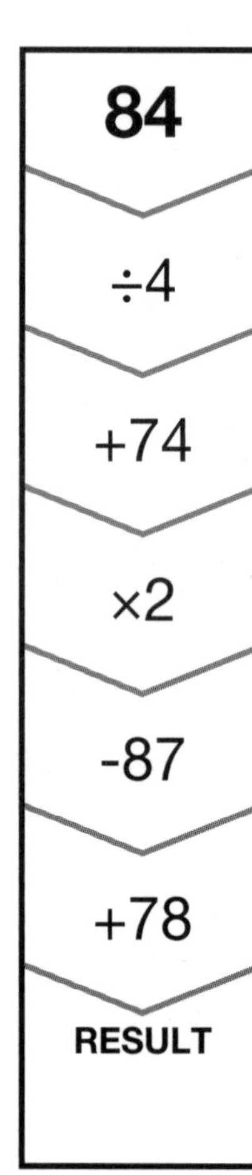

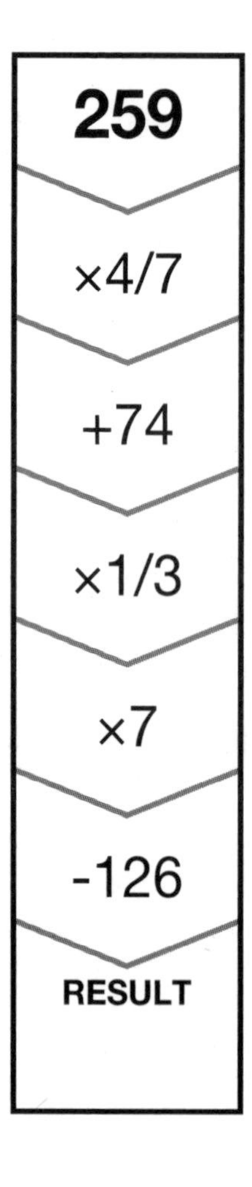

Word Orbit

By picking one letter from each orbit in turn, working in from the outermost ring to the innermost ring, how many four-letter words can you find?

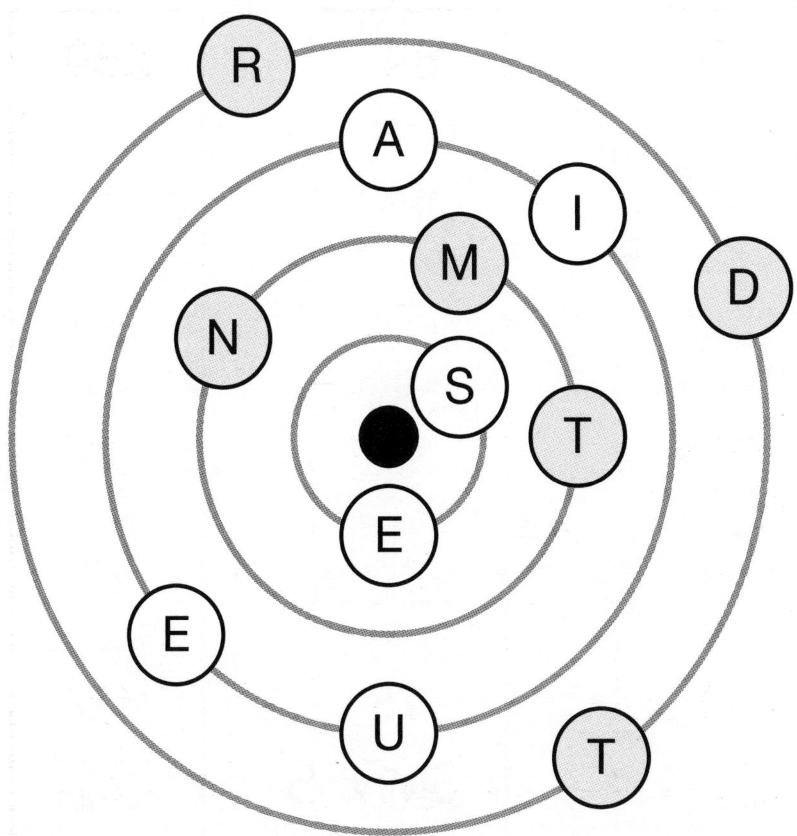

Missing Vowels

All of the vowels have been deleted from the following words. Can you restore them by working out what the original words were?

DRMR

QRRL

MNDFL

WNDRFL

WSMNSS

Hidden Path

Join some of the dots with horizontal and vertical lines to form a single path. The path should not touch or cross either itself or any of the solid blocks. Numbers outside the grid specify the exact number of dots in their row or column that are visited by the path. The start and end of the path are given to you, and are marked by the solid dots.

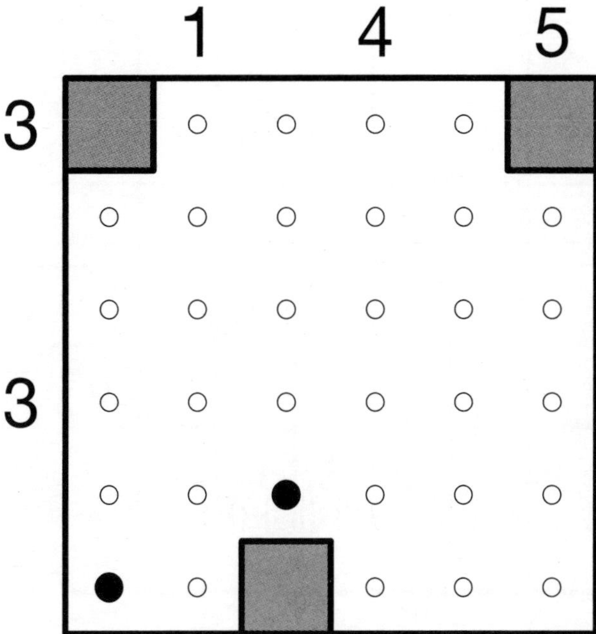

Binary Puzzle

Place a 0 or 1 in every empty square so that each row and column contains four '0's and four '1's. No more than two '0's or two '1's can appear consecutively in any row or column.

0	0		0	1		1	1
1			1	1			
	1				1	1	
0				1	1		
		0	1				0
	0	1				0	
			1	0			0
1	1		1	0		1	0

Grid Memory

Look at the pattern in the grid at the top-left of the page, then cover it over and see if you can accurately reproduce it in the empty grid at the top-right of the page. Then repeat with each of the other two grids.

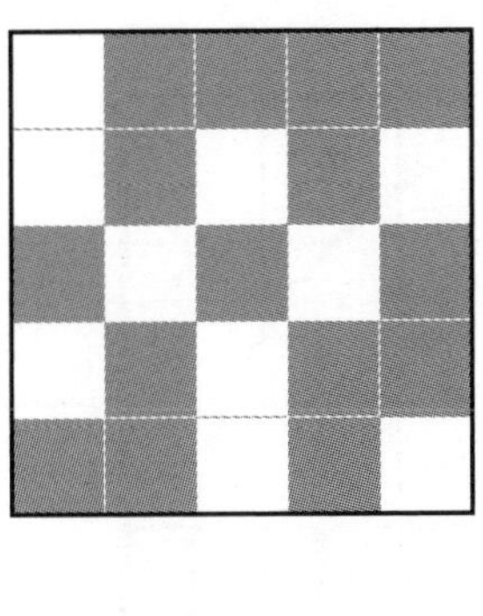

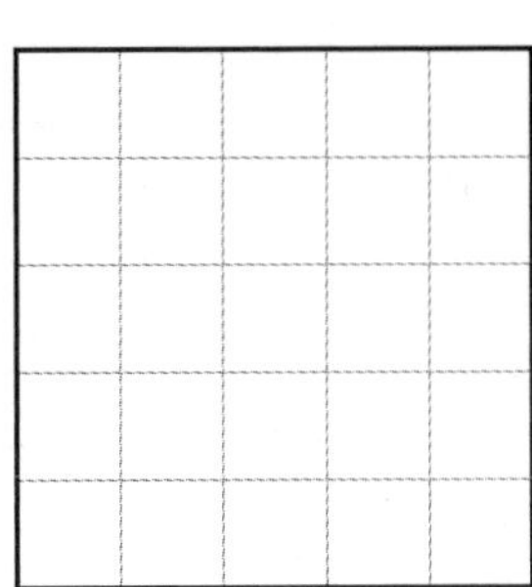

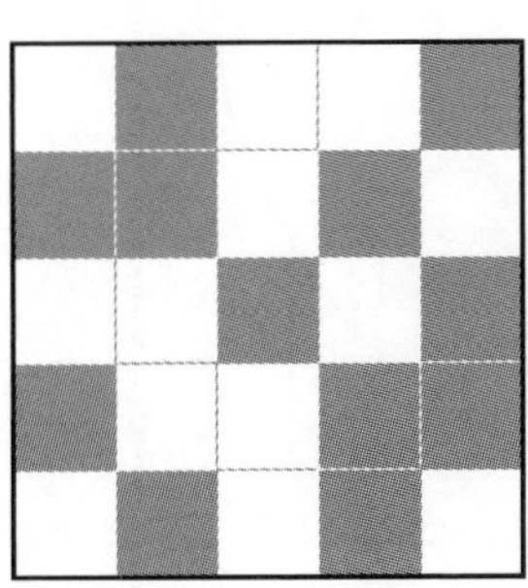

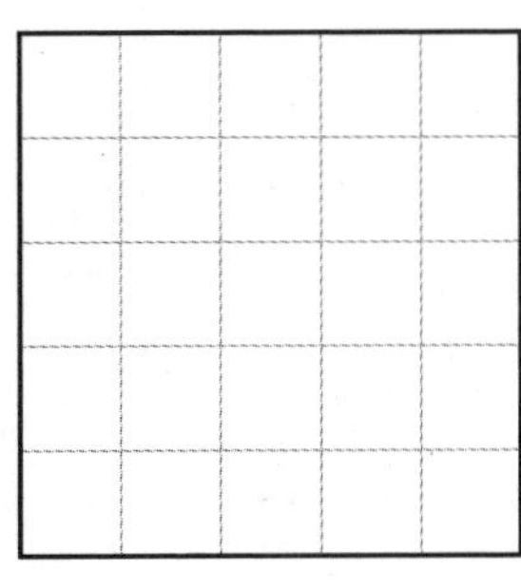

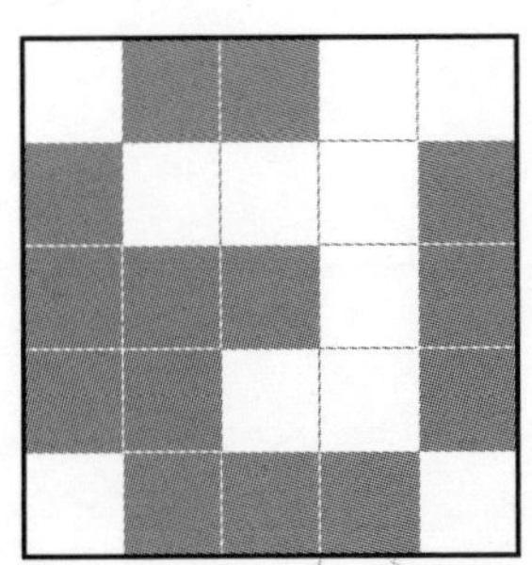

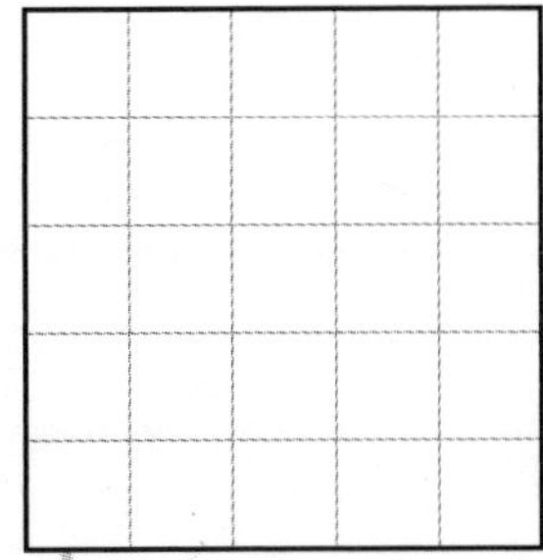

Letter Circle

How many words of three or more letters can you find in this letter circle? Each word should use the centre letter plus two or more of the other letters, and no letter can be used more than once in a single word. There is one word that uses every letter.

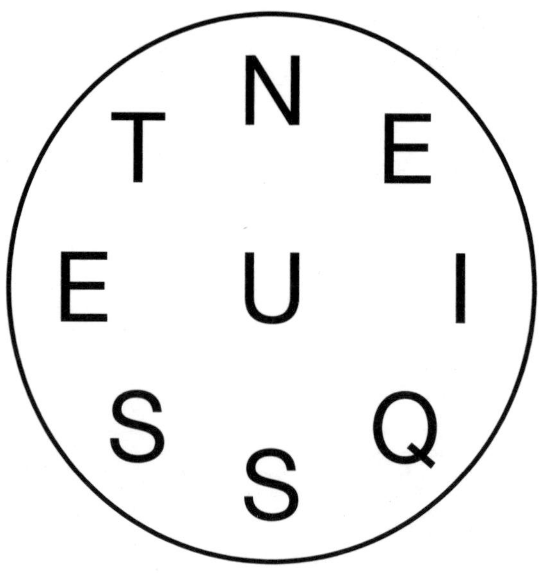

Fancy a challenge? If so, can you find 45 words?

Missing Signs

Give your mind a workout by writing the missing mathematical sign into each of these equations: +, −, × or ÷.

1 ☐ 21 = 22	17 ☐ 2 = 15
2 ☐ 16 = 18	36 ☐ 12 = 3
2 ☐ 17 = 19	59 ☐ 13 = 46
12 ☐ 12 = 144	73 ☐ 8 = 81
7 ☐ 17 = 24	14 ☐ 10 = 24
44 ☐ 19 = 63	15 ☐ 62 = 77
7 ☐ 12 = 19	40 ☐ 8 = 5
33 ☐ 4 = 29	132 ☐ 11 = 12
23 ☐ 10 = 13	3 ☐ 9 = 27
3 ☐ 5 = 15	36 ☐ 2 = 34

Dot Drawings

Try this creative task by drawing straight lines to join some, or all, of the dots together. See if you can come up with a pattern or picture, just with this restricted set of dots. Even if you have no idea what you want to draw, just start by joining dots at random and see what it begins to look like!

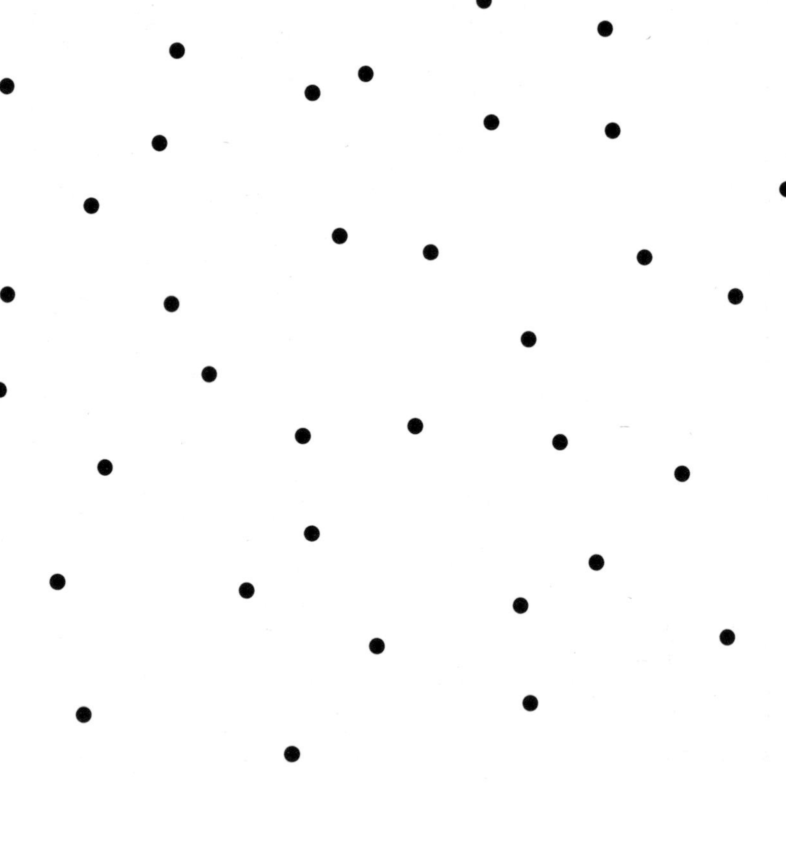

Number Link

Draw a series of separate paths, each connecting a pair of identical numbers. Paths only travel horizontally or vertically, and they don't cross or touch at any point. No more than one path can enter any grid square.

1			2	3		4		5	6
3									
							6		7
					8		9		
	1	2							
						8			
				9		4	5		
	10					10			
								7	

Futoshiki

Place 1 to 5 once each in every row and column, while obeying the greater-than signs – if there is a sign between two squares, then the arrow always points at the smaller of the two numbers.

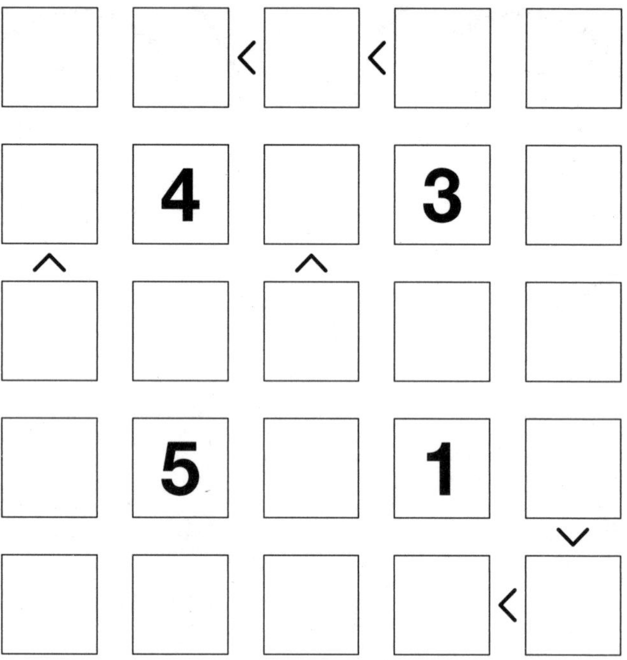

Magic Square

Create your own optical illusion by tracing over the light grey parts of these circles with a bold red pen, or any other vivid colour. What do you see? Does it now look like there's a coloured square in the middle?

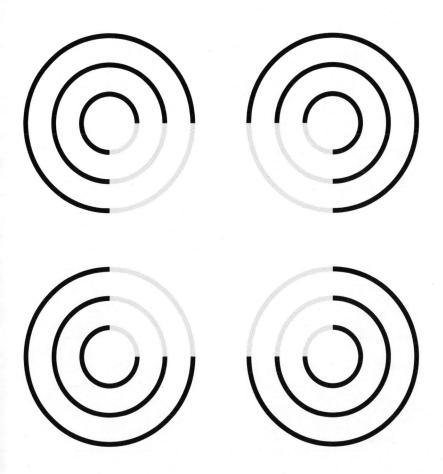

Missing Vegetables

First, cover up the bottom of the page (below the dividing line), then spend up to a minute remembering the list of vegetables below, then cover it over, wait a few seconds, and then see if you can spot which ones are missing from the list at the bottom of the page.

Artichoke	Lettuce	Marrow
Courgette	Cabbage	Beetroot
Leek	Spinach	Turnip
Onion	Sweetcorn	Garlic
Celery	Asparagus	Carrot

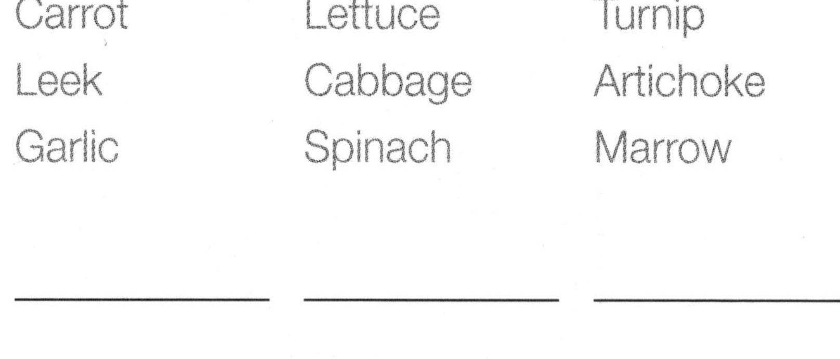

Carrot	Lettuce	Turnip
Leek	Cabbage	Artichoke
Garlic	Spinach	Marrow

__________ __________ __________

__________ __________ __________

Jigsaw Letters

To solve these puzzles, place a letter from A to E in each empty square so that every row, column and bold-lined jigsaw shape contains each letter exactly once.

Puzzle 1

	C		E	
		D		
	D		B	

Puzzle 2

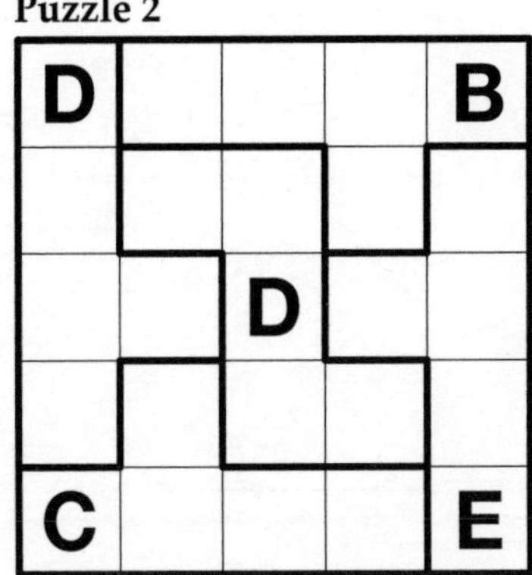

Mini Crossword

Solve each of the clues to complete this mini-crossword grid.

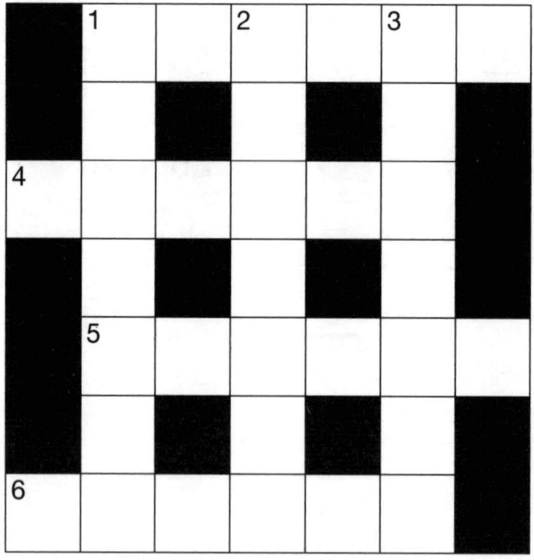

Across
1 Goes up a ladder (6)
4 Screenplay (6)
5 Prone (6)
6 Tabs (6)

Down
1 Spiral ear cavity (7)
2 Copy (7)
3 Glass containers (7)

Mental Maths

Massage your brain with these maths calculations – do as many as you can without using a calculator or making written notes.

$32 - 22 =$	$28 + 24 =$
$12 \times 11 =$	$36 + 20 =$
$26 - 9 =$	$4 \times 8 =$
$17 + 86 =$	$31 - 8 =$
$10 + 55 =$	$12 + 23 =$
$28 - 10 =$	$189 \div 3 =$
$5 \times 15 =$	$10 + 6 =$
$192 \div 12 =$	$10 \times 4 =$
$65 - 6 =$	$96 - 25 =$
$84 - 10 =$	$27 + 27 =$

Beach Confusion

Each of the following phrases can be rearranged to form the name of something you might bring to the beach. Can you solve them all?

ARID CHECK

USES SLANGS

I SUMS WIT

NOR ELKS

ROBS FRAUD

Silhouette Selection

Which of the four silhouettes matches the leaves at the top of the page?

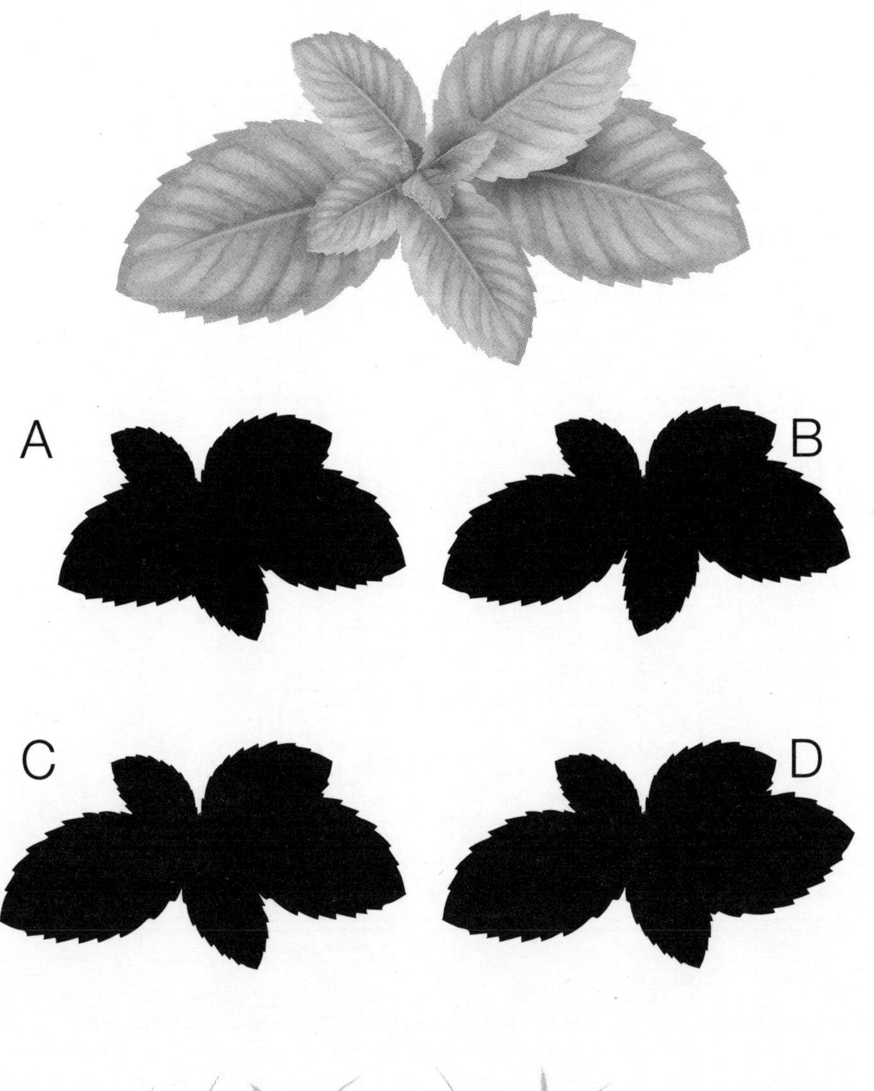

Classic Maze

Can you find your way through this square maze, travelling from the entrance at the top all the way down to the exit at the bottom?

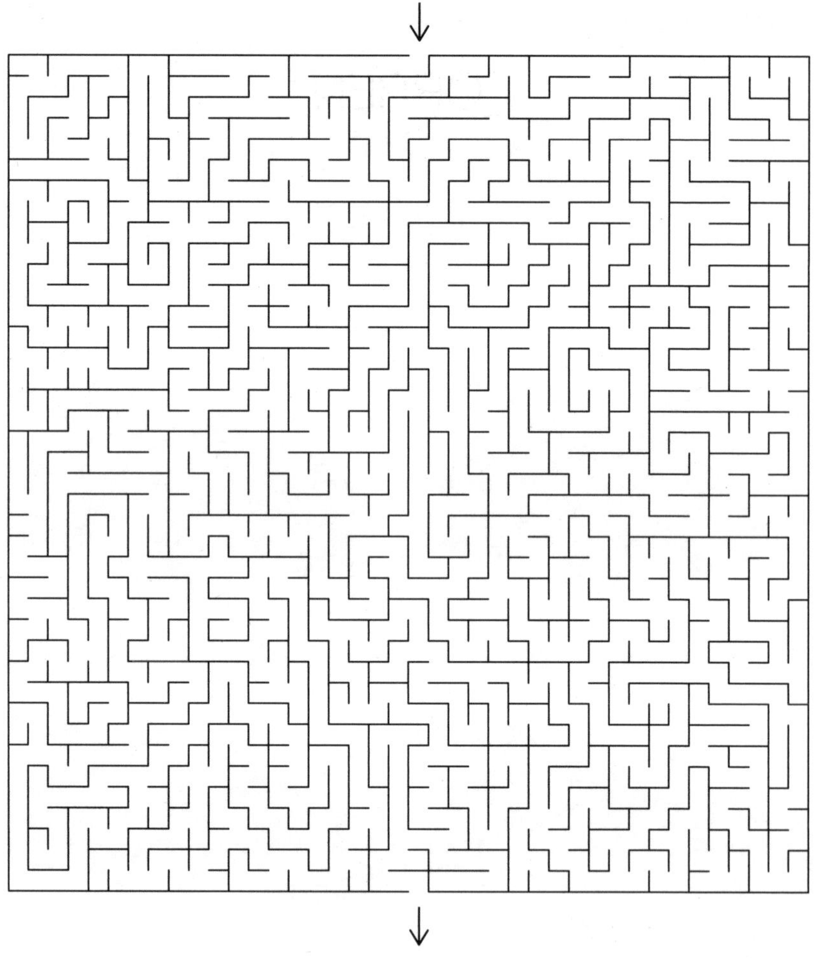

Start and End

For each of these puzzles, add the same letter to both the start and end of the given fragment to form a normal English word. For example, add S to _TART_ to form STARTS.

ORREN

WARD

AYBE

OPCOA

RMAD

YNI

AUNC

Image Combination

Imagine combining these two images, so each white square in one is filled with the contents of the corresponding square in the other image. How many circles would there be in total?

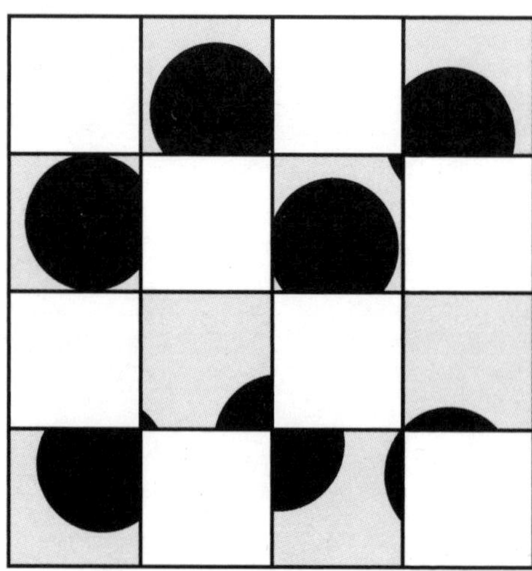

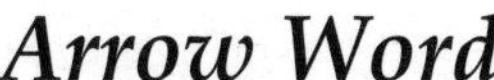

Arrow Word

All of this crossword's clues are given inside the grid.

Lower down		Healthy vegetable dish?		Browse the Web		Arrive at		Teaching
Announces formally		Hundreds of years		Hot drink dispensers				
								Ogle
Climbing plant, sweet —				Destiny				
Objective				Will Ferrell Christmas film	Loud shout			
			Wall-climbing lizard		Colour			
Works of creative imagination	Unsightly					Pond organism		Largest Australian birds
In fashion	Sports arbiter				Had lunch			
				Thin and graceful				
Plus	Just manage to make				African antelope			
				Graffiti identifiers				

Cube Counting

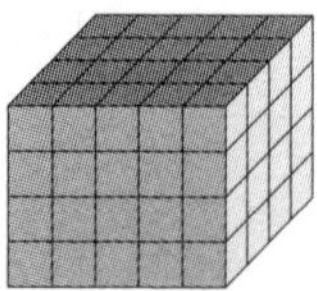

How many individual cubes have been used to build the structure below? You should assume that all 'hidden' cubes are present, and that it started off as a perfect 5×4×4 arrangement of cubes (as shown to the right) before any cubes were removed. There are no floating cubes.

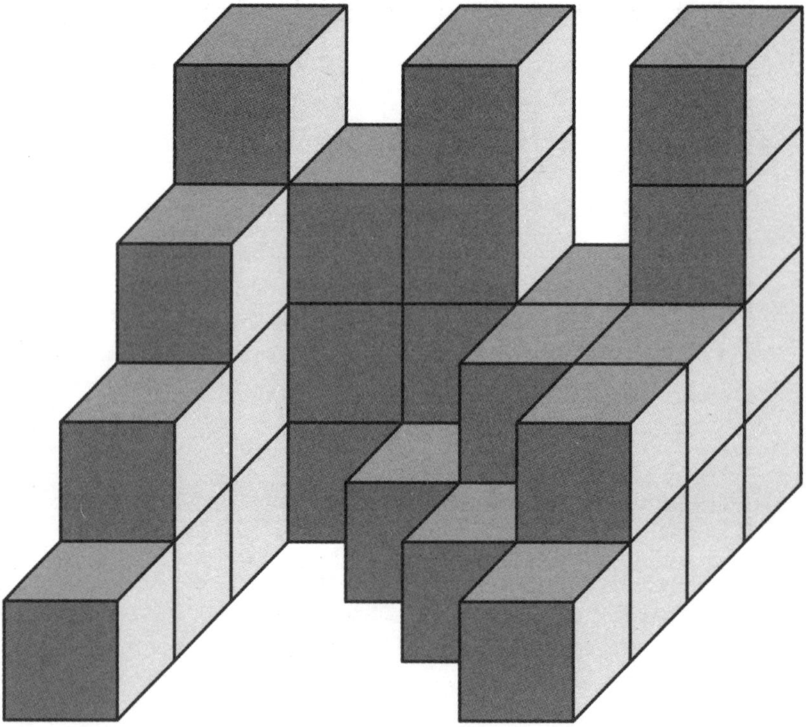

Island Groups

Can you find all of the listed entries in the grid? They are written forwards or backwards in any direction, including diagonally.

```
I E M S M O F S I G N I P L A
A O R I E Y T L A Y O L I O I
I A B B C N G I S M S C N D L
S T R A A R I Y E I O E A N E
A U I I E I O P I W C A I A O
I V T S I N S N P G A G I I R
I A I E E A A E E I N C A N I
N L S N A O C E N S L S W O A
L U H Y I O S I G A I I A I B
U I V L C I E G R E L A H R S
A R I O Y R I P I A A E E P I
T A R P I A I T N J E M M O F
I A G D R A W E E L I L M N I
I E I E E N A E A G F F A M L
C A N A R Y A E O L I A N B U
```

AEGEAN
AEOLIAN
BALEARIC
BRITISH VIRGIN
CANARY
FIJI
HAWAIIAN
IONIAN
LEEWARD
LOYALTY
MELANESIA
MICRONESIA
PHILIPPINE
POLYNESIA
SAMOA
TUVALU

Boxing Away

Fit all the listed words into the grid, crossword-style.

4 Letters
Quit
Sigh
Test
Uses

5 Letters
Adder
Casts
Spike
Steed
Swims
Tasks

6 Letters
Carbon
Clergy
Crying
Hernia
Noodle
System

7 Letters
Cheaply
Implied
Ostrich
Relying
Sausage
Scratch
Turning
Upsilon

11 Letters
Cholesterol
Repertoires

Word Sliders

How many five-letter words can you spell out using the sliders? One word is spelled out for you already. Each slider can be slid up or down to reveal a single letter.

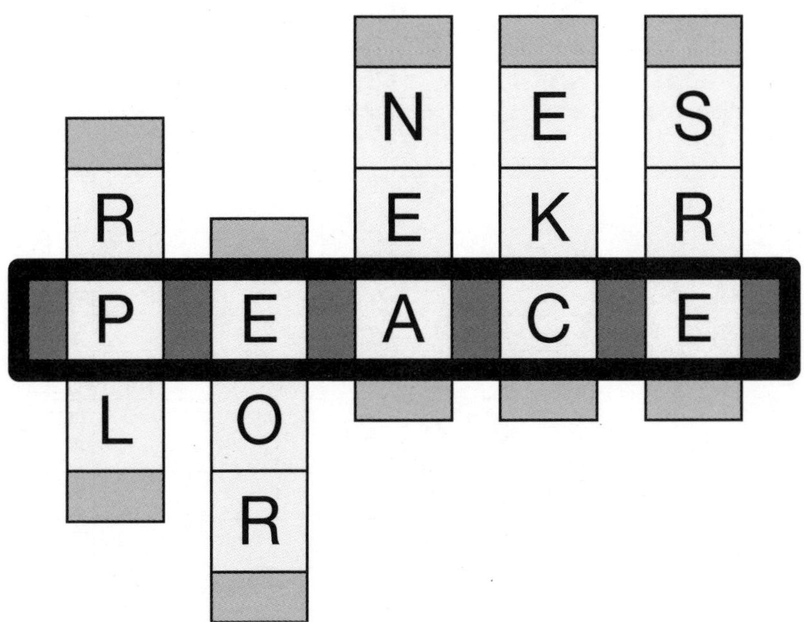

Pretty

Colour this image using the number key below – what appears?

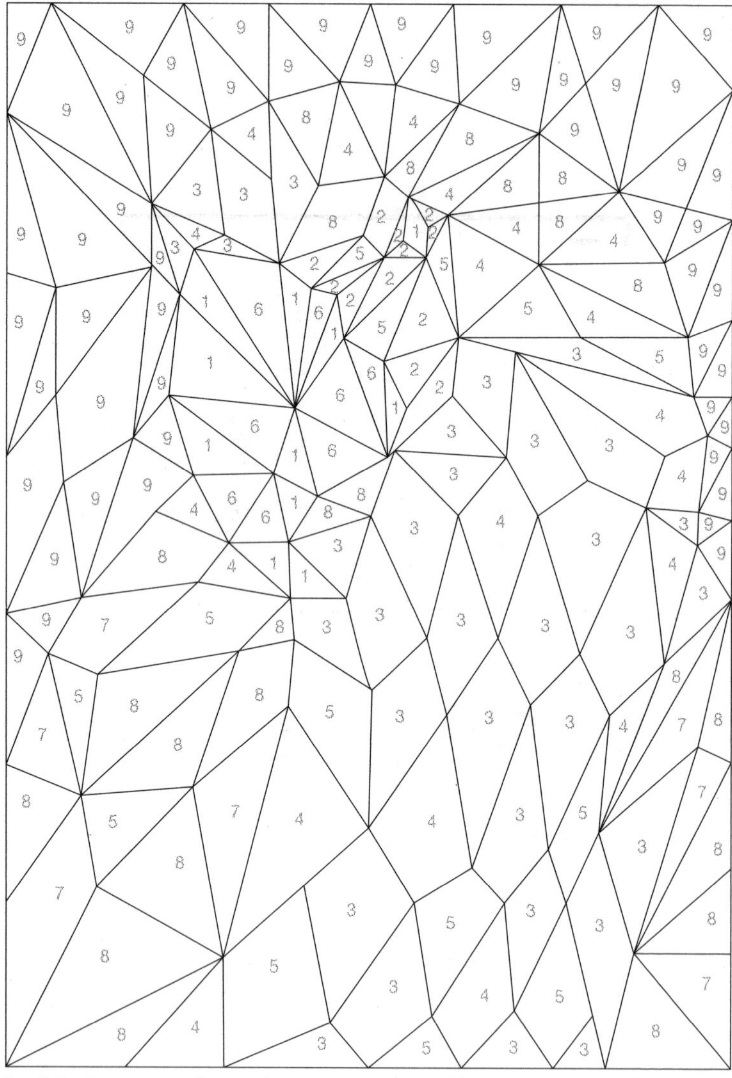

1 – black
2 – white
3 – red
4 – orange
5 – yellow
6 – grey
7 – royal blue
8 – dark green

Touchy Letters

Place one letter from A to F into every empty box, so that each row and column contains all six different letters. Also, identical letters can't be in touching boxes – not even diagonally.

F					A
		F	A		
	D			F	
	F			D	
		E	C		
C					E

Minesweeper

Can you work out where the hidden mines are? Some of the empty squares contain mines – mark them in. Clues in some squares show the number of mines in touching squares, including diagonally touching squares. No more than one mine may be placed per square.

	1				1
2		3		4	
	3		3		2
	5		3	2	
	4				1
1				1	

Order Recall

First, cover up the bottom of the page (below the dividing line), then spend up to a minute remembering the order of the list of gym kit below, then cover it over, wait a few seconds, and then see if you can recall the order that the kit was in. You'll be given the list again.

1. Mat
2. Step
3. Dumb-bell
4. Bench
5. Treadmill
6. Beams
7. Ab wheel
8. Barbell
9. Rope
10. Ball
11. Leg press
12. Bars
13. Leg curl
14. Rower
15. Weight

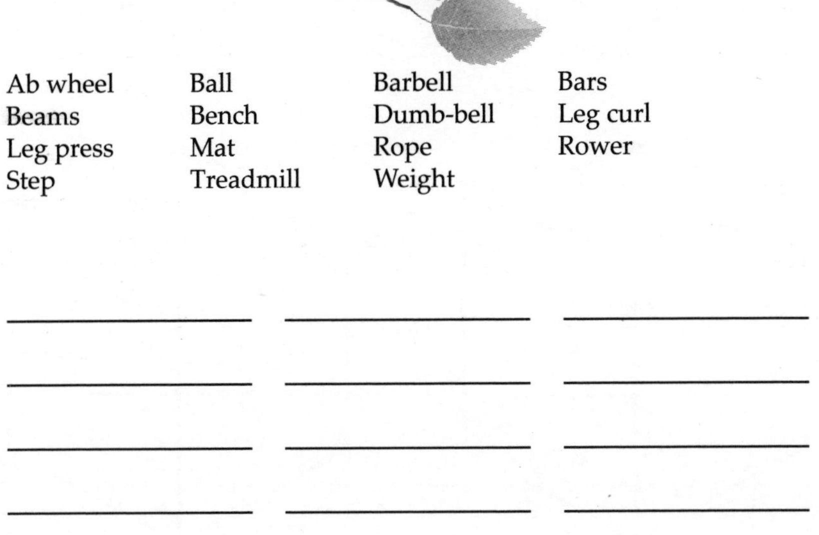

Ab wheel	Ball	Barbell	Bars
Beams	Bench	Dumb-bell	Leg curl
Leg press	Mat	Rope	Rower
Step	Treadmill	Weight	

______________	______________	______________
______________	______________	______________
______________	______________	______________
______________	______________	______________
______________	______________	______________

Creative Cubing

Using your imagination, can you use a pen or pencil to convert these cubes into pictures of four different **ways you might gift-wrap or decorate a box**? For example, one could have an elaborate bow.

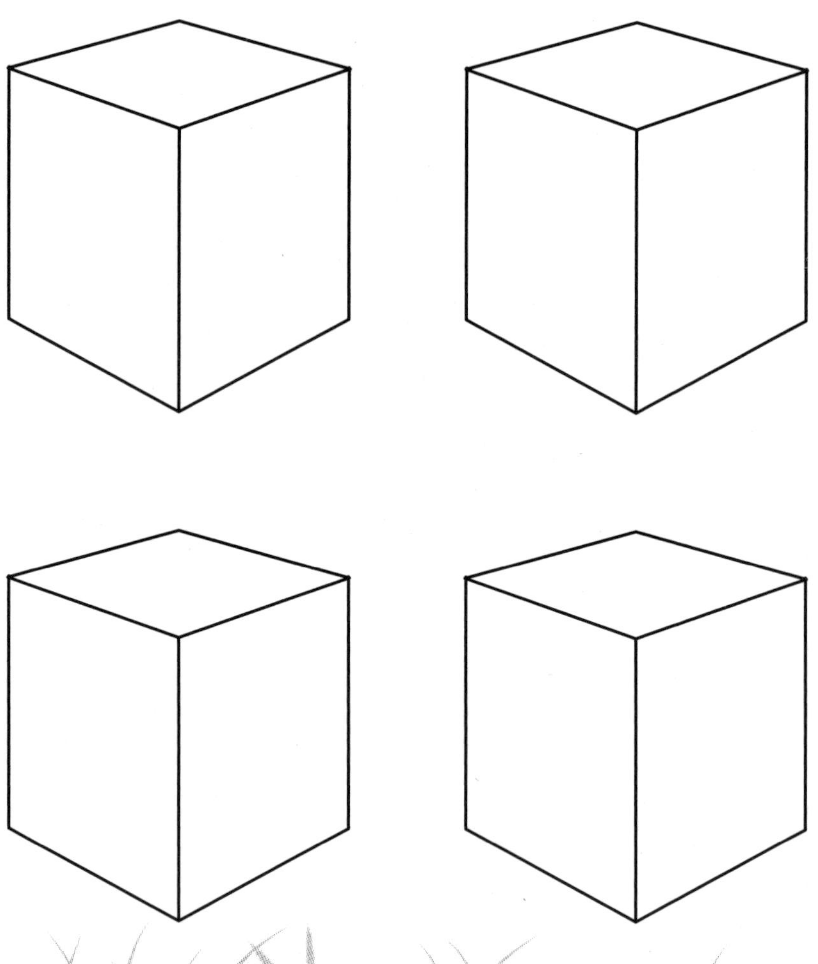

Deleted Letters

Delete one letter from each touching pair of letters to reveal four hidden words, one per row. For example, CD AL TM would lead to C~~D~~ A~~L~~ T~~M~~, revealing CAT.

MW IO DR PD

RP UI NP LP YE

BD OR RN LU SM

CD RL AI AM MA ET NE

Word Paths

How many words of three or more letters can you find in this square? Find words by moving horizontally or vertically (but not diagonally) from letter to touching letter, and without revisiting a square in a single word. There is also one word that uses every letter.

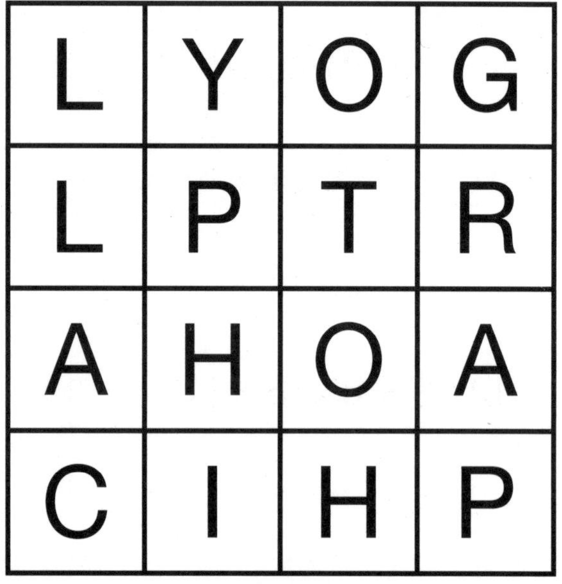

L	Y	O	G
L	P	T	R
A	H	O	A
C	I	H	P

Fancy a challenge? If so, can you find 20 words?

Time Totals

Exercise your mind with these time calculations. Just add the two times, or subtract the second time from the first as appropriate.

22:35 - 18:20 =	:
23:40 - 21:50 =	:
07:25 + 06:05 =	:
11:00 + 06:10 =	:
13:20 - 05:15 =	:
09:55 + 04:20 =	:
02:25 - 01:10 =	:
21:50 - 03:50 =	:
09:35 + 07:40 =	:
12:40 + 09:15 =	:

Principal Target

Can you transform CORE into AIMS in just five steps? At each step you should change a single letter to form a new word, but without rearranging the order of any of the letters. For example, you could start by stepping from CORE to CODE, and then from CODE to NODE.

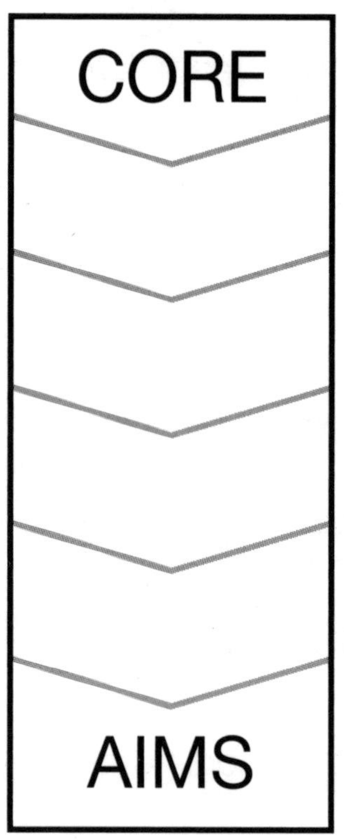

Rhyming Lines

See if you can come up with a rhyming second line for each of these extremely brief poems – the more ridiculous the better!

In every dream I've ever had,

____

My winter wonder wanders wide,

____

In the middle of a muddle,

____

Simple Loop

Draw a single loop that visits every empty square once each, using just horizontal and vertical lines.

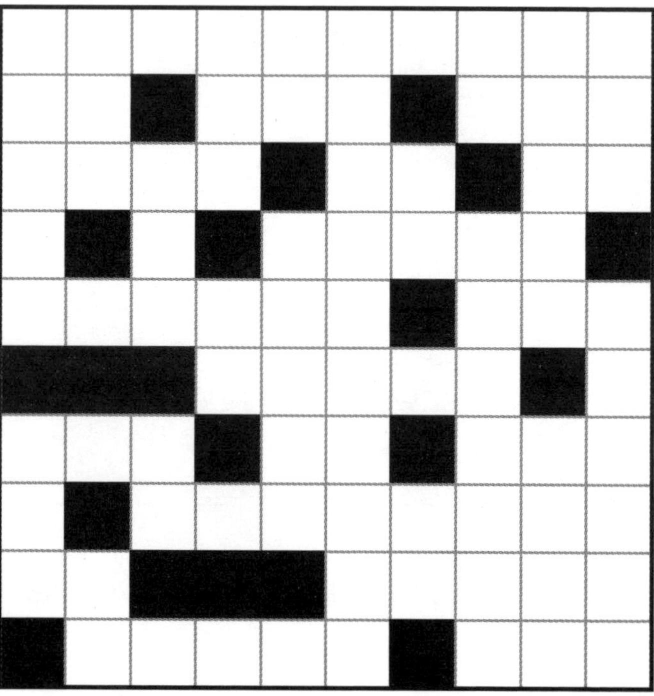

Letter Circle

How many words of three or more letters can you find in this letter circle? Each word should use the centre letter plus two or more of the other letters, and no letter can be used more than once in a single word. There is one word that uses every letter.

Fancy a challenge? If so, can you find 35 words?

Missing Signs

Give your mind a workout by writing the missing mathematical sign into each of these equations: +, −, × or ÷.

27	☐	5	=	32	4	☐	12	=	48
60	☐	10	=	6	28	☐	4	=	32
28	☐	3	=	25	63	☐	11	=	52
24	☐	6	=	4	2	☐	10	=	20
49	☐	7	=	7	72	☐	12	=	6
3	☐	4	=	12	3	☐	5	=	15
7	☐	4	=	11	12	☐	15	=	27
6	☐	6	=	36	41	☐	11	=	30
7	☐	5	=	35	62	☐	6	=	56
17	☐	69	=	86	7	☐	8	=	56

Word Fit

Fit all the listed words into the grid, crossword-style.

3 Letters
Dud
Via

4 Letters
Deli
Fete
Firm
Rear

5 Letters
Amuse
Demon
Their
Throb

6 Letters
Agenda
Balsam
Detest
Oddity
Satire
Sports

7 Letters
Deficit
Pulling
Scarlet
Sillier

8 Letters
Flabbily
Gladioli
Outlined
Vehicles

9 Letters
Abolishes
Manifesto

Every Other Letter

In the following list of elemental gases, every other letter has been removed. Can you restore the missing letters to reveal the full set of gases?

_Y_R_G_N

O_Y_E_

_R_P_O_

_H_O_I_E

_E_N

Hourglass Maze

Can you find your way through this hourglass-shaped maze, travelling from the entrance at the top all the way down to the exit at the bottom?

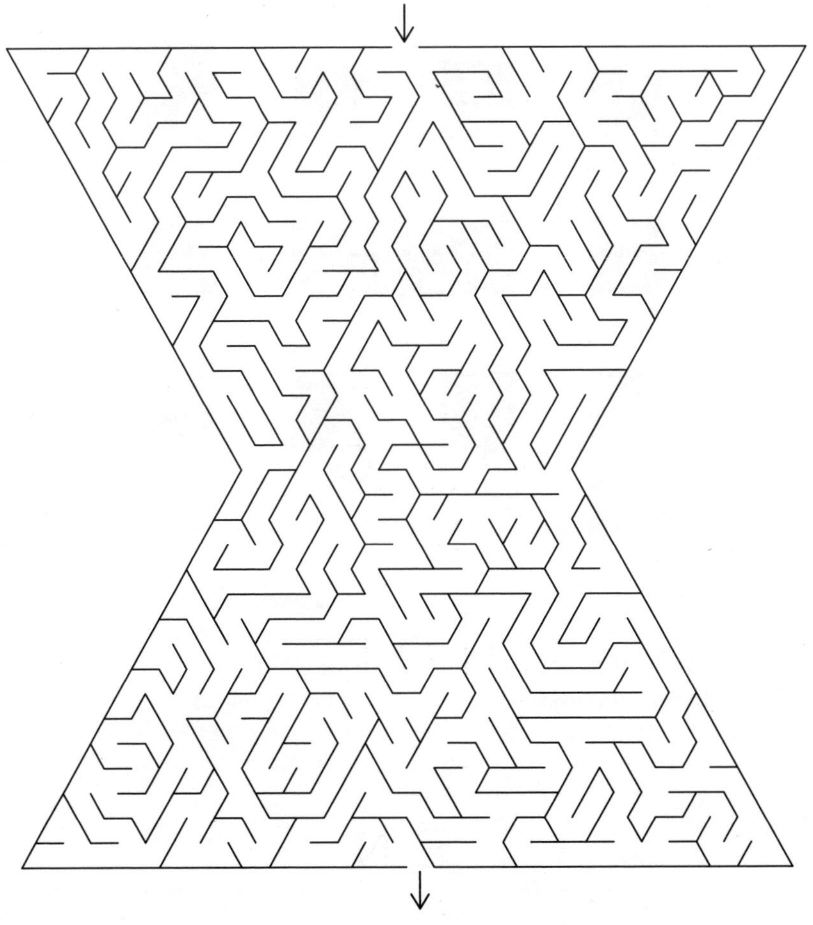

Mini Crossword

Solve each of the clues to complete this mini-crossword grid.

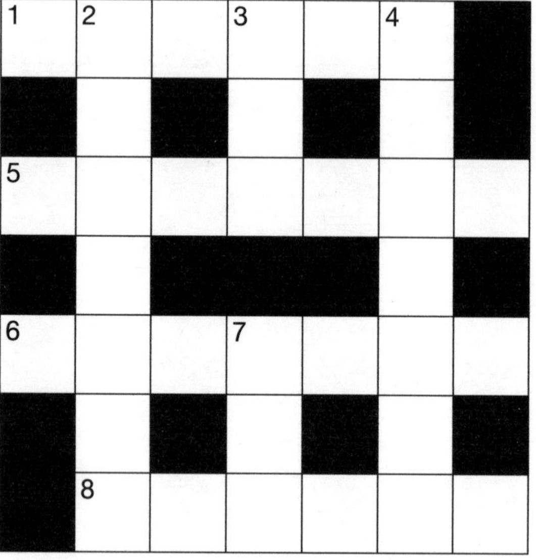

Across

1 Arachnid (6)
5 Insurance payment (7)
6 Trattoria dumplings (7)
8 Matrices (6)

Down

2 Predatory South American fish (7)
3 Faintly lit (3)
4 Approximately (7)
7 Beetle or Polo, eg (3)

Mental Maths

Massage your brain with these maths calculations – do as many as you can without using a calculator or making written notes.

$84 - 25 =$ ☐	$23 + 99 =$ ☐
$171 \div 9 =$ ☐	$46 - 22 =$ ☐
$51 - 19 =$ ☐	$7 \times 5 =$ ☐
$67 - 12 =$ ☐	$136 \div 2 =$ ☐
$3 \times 4 =$ ☐	$22 + 77 =$ ☐
$10 \times 18 =$ ☐	$8 + 90 =$ ☐
$17 + 48 =$ ☐	$84 - 29 =$ ☐
$73 - 28 =$ ☐	$22 + 73 =$ ☐
$192 \div 3 =$ ☐	$13 + 26 =$ ☐
$42 - 25 =$ ☐	$5 \times 3 =$ ☐

Rectangles and Squares

Draw along some of the dashed lines to divide the grid into a set of rectangles and squares, so that every rectangle or square contains exactly one number. That number must always be equal to the number of grid squares within the rectangle or square.

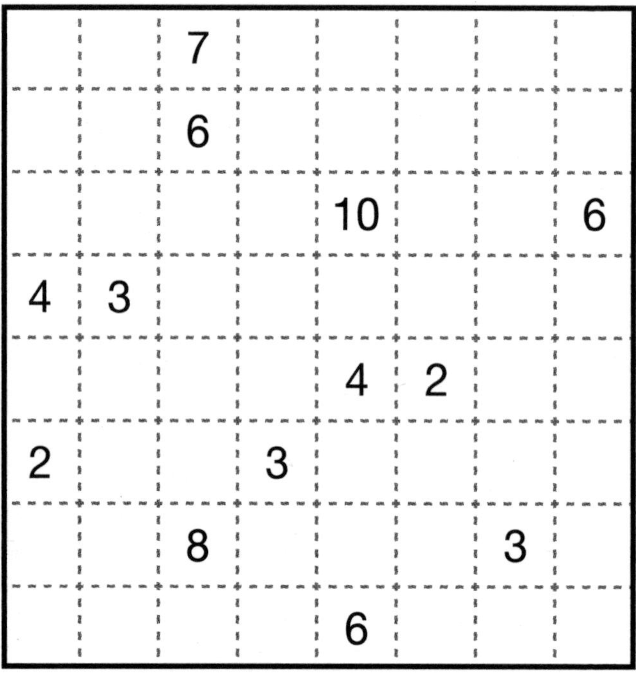

Link Words

Find a common English word to place in each gap, so that both when attached to the end of the first word and when attached to the start of the second word you end up with two more English words. For example, **birth** _ _ _ **break** could be solved using **day**, making **birthday** and **daybreak**.

off _ _ _ box

sun _ _ _ going

fore _ _ _ _ _ _ _ _ fully

Animal Sightings

Can you find all of the listed animals in the grid? They are written forwards or backwards in any direction, including diagonally.

S	H	L	R	E	R	M	E	A	A	L	R	L	A	H
L	C	E	S	E	G	S	R	T	E	A	R	S	O	O
B	G	L	S	H	R	G	N	B	B	A	N	A	E	B
C	R	A	M	O	E	L	H	B	O	O	N	O	F	E
E	L	E	H	L	L	E	I	I	K	D	S	L	F	A
T	R	A	I	T	L	T	P	N	O	P	E	E	A	V
M	H	O	M	A	A	M	I	G	E	N	A	E	R	E
O	N	E	M	A	M	L	A	A	B	E	W	L	I	R
U	I	E	A	N	A	I	F	E	A	H	R	E	G	U
S	M	O	N	K	E	Y	A	P	E	R	H	P	C	C
E	R	A	L	L	I	R	O	G	E	M	R	H	S	A
D	I	E	E	E	N	A	R	M	S	I	L	A	A	M
B	Y	T	A	R	L	B	B	A	B	T	L	N	L	E
N	A	L	B	S	A	O	B	T	R	L	G	T	E	L
C	O	G	W	O	C	A	B	E	E	B	O	B	E	I

BEAR
BEAVER
CAMEL
CAT
COW
DOG
ELEPHANT
GIRAFFE
GORILLA
HORSE
LION
LLAMA
MONKEY
MOUSE
RABBIT
SHEEP

Brain Chains

Can you solve each of the three brain chains completely in your head, without making any written notes? Start with the bold number at the top, and then apply each maths operation in turn. Write your final result in at the bottom.

5
+49
-39
+15
×1/3
-8
RESULT

77
-28
×6/7
-1
+44
÷5
RESULT

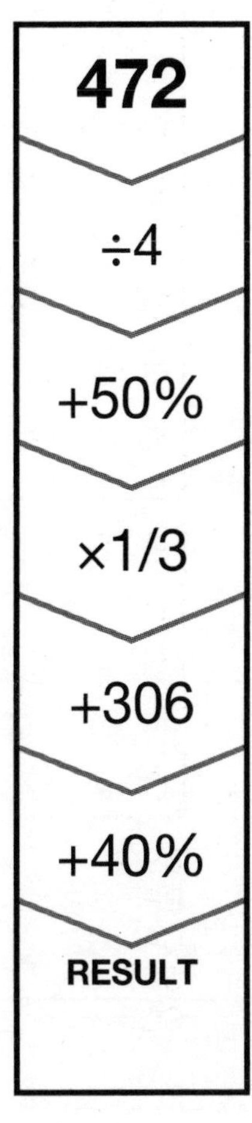

Arrow Word

All of this crossword's clues are given inside the grid.

Royal castle governor		Medical centre		Cover		Extremely destructive type of weapon		Zone
Unlimited		Conifer		US TV show, 'My Name is ___'				
								Travelled through the air
One of seven deadly things				Noggin				
Stumble					Father		Extents	
Car anti-skid program (inits)		Touch or taste		Remove fat from milk				
			Malevolence		Harsh bird cry			
Onion relative					Mineral spring	High, snow-capped peak		Prior to (archaic)
Conceive of								
Fight to settle an issue of honour	Less complex							
				Semicircular church recess				

Missing Items

First, cover up the bottom of the page (below the dividing line), then spend up to a minute remembering the list of currencies below, then cover it over, wait a few seconds, and then see if you can spot which ones are missing from the list at the bottom of the page.

Won	Pound	Zloty
Lira	Kuna	Yuan
Yen	Dram	Dinar
Baht	Drachma	Euro
Dollar	Guilder	Krone

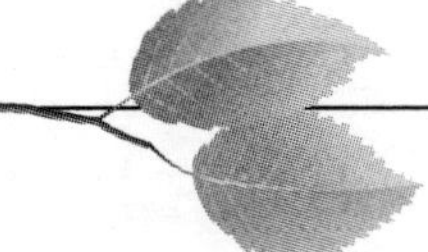

Pound	Drachma	Dinar
Baht	Kuna	Yen
Guilder	Euro	Yuan

__________ __________ __________

__________ __________ __________

Aerial Movement

Rearrange each set of boxes to spell out a series of constellations.

Puzzle 1

S	RI	AQ	U	UA

Puzzle 2

SA	TTA	US	RI	GI

Puzzle 3

IA	IO	SS	PE	CA

Puzzle 4

ED	AN	OM	A	DR

Triangular Tussle

Colour these impossible triangles as you please, although if you use three contrasting shades of the same colour for each triangle then you may create an even more convincing – yet still impossible – 3D shape!

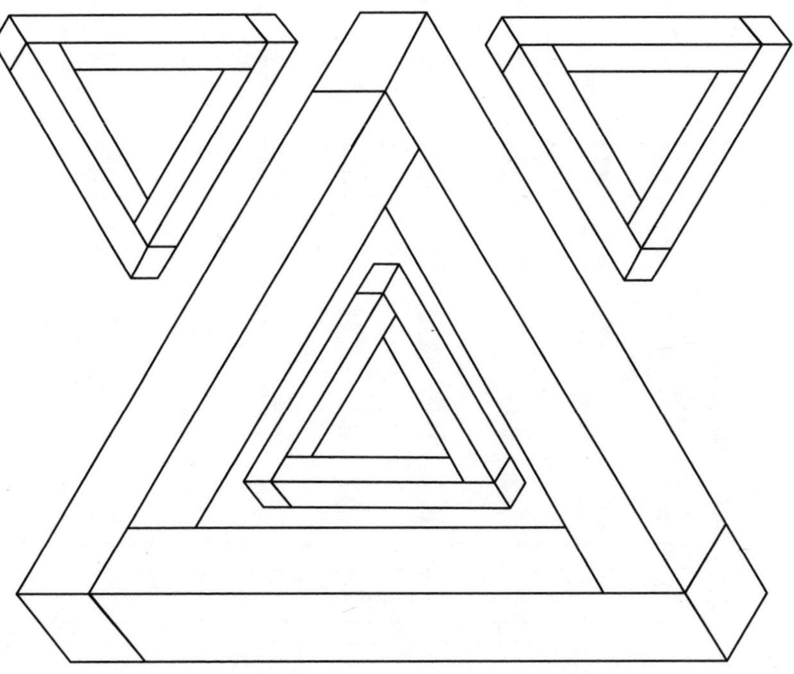

Domino Set

Draw solid lines to divide the grid into a full set of standard dominoes, with exactly one of each domino. A '0' represents a blank on a traditional domino. Use the check-off chart to help you keep track of which dominoes you've placed.

6	6	2	4	5	6	0	0
0	1	3	3	2	1	1	5
3	0	4	6	4	4	1	4
3	2	5	2	1	4	5	2
2	6	0	3	5	1	5	0
6	0	5	2	4	6	1	1
5	0	3	2	6	4	3	3

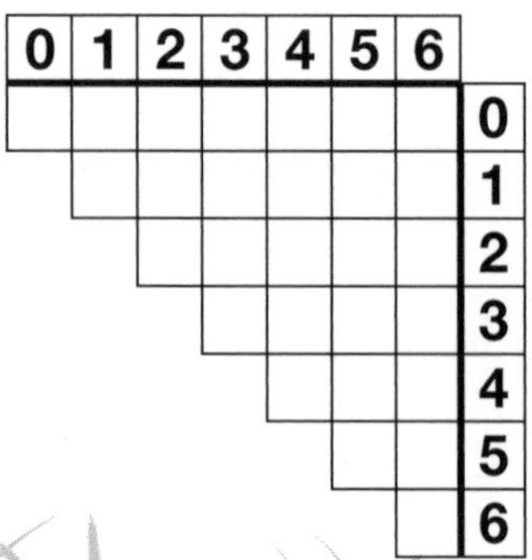

Country Confusions

Each of the following phrases can be rearranged to form the name of a country. Can you solve them all?

AN IDLER

ULTRA ASIA

GUT POLAR

GIANT NEAR

MEG RYAN

Missing Vowels

All of the vowels have been deleted from the following words. Can you restore them by working out what the original words were?

XTRM

CQRD

STRNT

BRVTY

XC

Something to Find

Can you transform SEEK into THIS in just five steps? At each step you should change a single letter to form a new word, but without rearranging the order of any of the letters. For example, you could start by stepping from SEEK to SEED, and then from SEED to SHED.

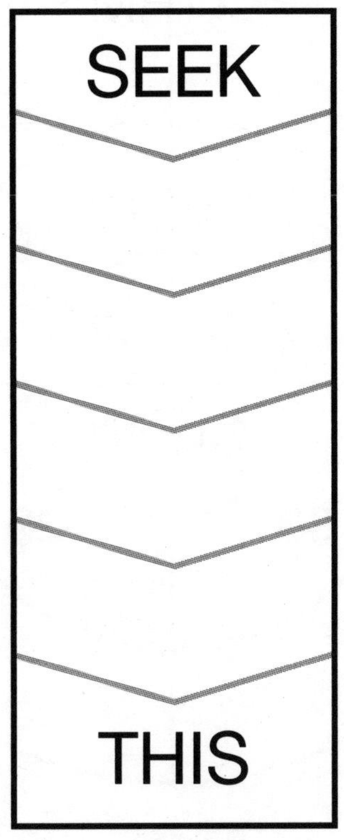

Number Darts

Can you make each of the totals shown below this number dartboard? For each total, choose one number from the inner ring, one number from the middle ring, and one number from the outer ring. The three numbers must add to the given total.

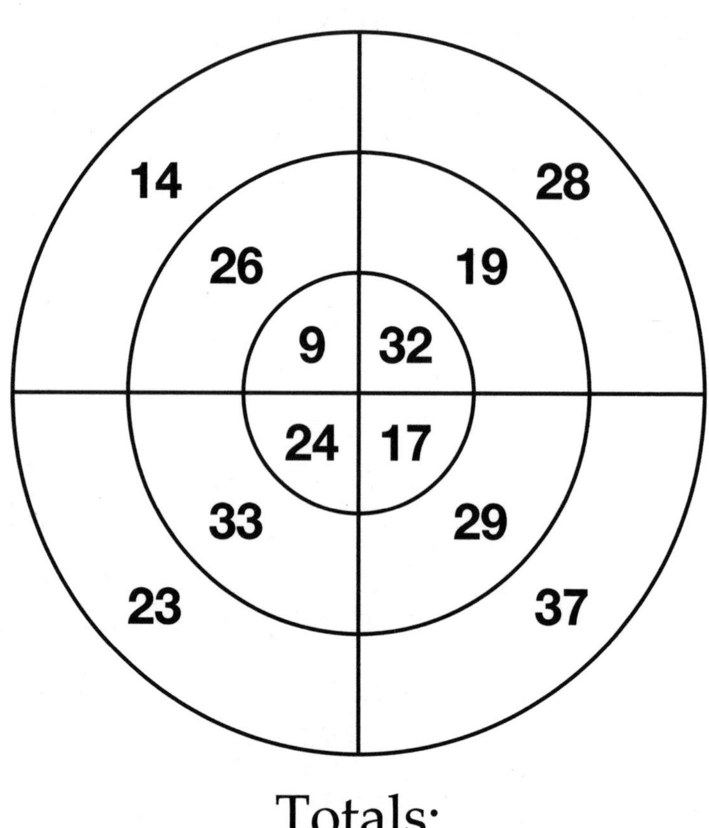

Totals:

50 70 90

Looking at the Clouds

Can you find all of the listed types of cloud in the grid? Words are written forwards or backwards in any direction, including diagonally.

```
T S P S U L U M U C O T L A T
F U I U L A C U N O S U S T S
L T L I A A R C U S A L U U S
M A E C O A S U S L S S C U P
U R U I A R S U U U T A U Y C
U T S S T S R U T L P U R T S
F S T I U R T A T O L O U S N
E O U P I N R E A A C A U I V
O R T C A T I S L U L C L E U
U R S L S S U C M L N U L L I
I I U O T S S U N I A U D T C
S C T I P U L I U U M N S N N
O L U L T U E S S N U E U U U
A L E L S S U T A R B I F S N
M A L I N T O R T U S T N A S
```

ALTOCUMULUS
ALTOSTRATUS
ARCUS
CASTELLANUS
CIRROSTRATUS
CIRRUS
FIBRATUS
INCUS
INTORTUS
LACUNOSUS
OPACUS
PILEUS
PYROCUMULUS
UNCINUS
UNDULATUS
VELUM

Anagram Pairs

Draw lines to join each word in the left-hand column to a word in the right-hand column, where the two words are anagrams of one another. For example, you could join MELONS to LEMONS.

Detour	Organs
Drawer	Paging
Gaping	Pedant
Groans	Planes
Leased	Rename
Luring	Routed
Meaner	Routes
Nested	Ruling
Neural	Sealed
Opuses	Spares
Ouster	Spouse
Palest	Staple
Panels	Tensed
Panted	Unreal
Parses	Warred

Word Paths

How many words of three or more letters can you find in this square? Find words by moving horizontally or vertically (but not diagonally) from letter to touching letter, and without revisiting a square in a single word. There is also one word that uses every letter.

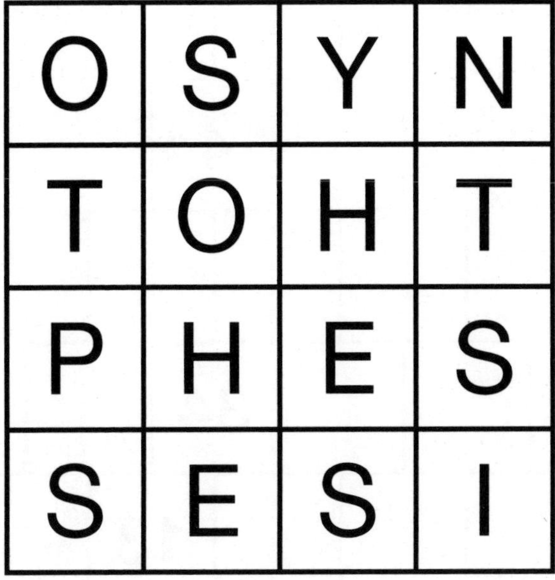

O	S	Y	N
T	O	H	T
P	H	E	S
S	E	S	I

Fancy a challenge? If so, can you find 15 words?

Number Pyramid

Write a number in every empty block so that each block is equal to the sum of the two blocks directly beneath it.

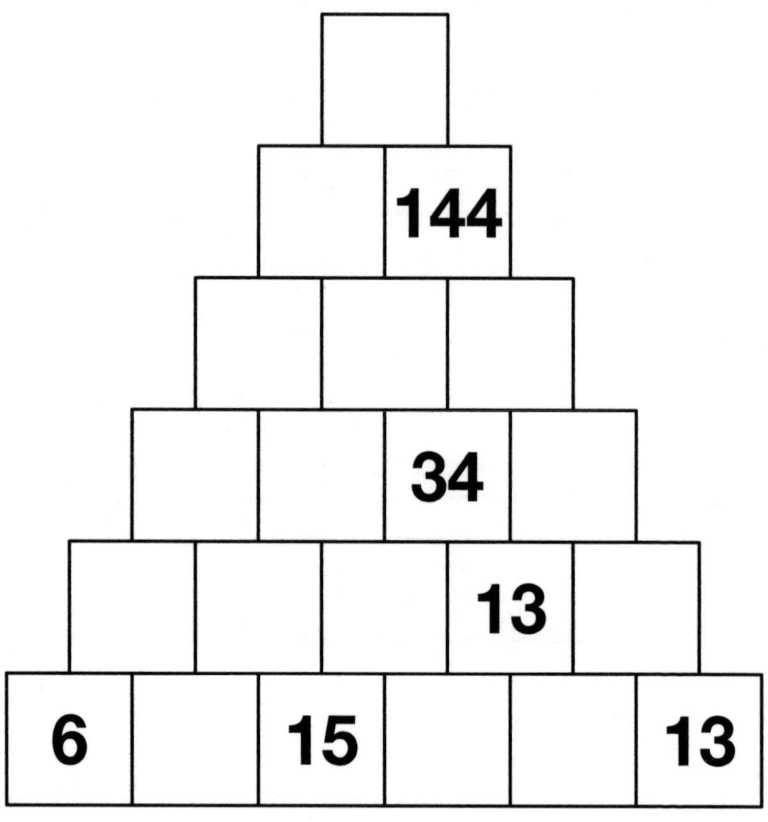

Reverse Words

Can you solve each of the following clues? Each pair of clues reveal the same word, except that the solution to each 'b' clue is the **reverse** of the 'a' clue. For example, if the 'a' solution is DOG then the 'b' solution will be GOD, and vice versa.

Puzzle 1
a. Doe or roe
b. Water grass

Puzzle 2
a. Items of cutlery
b. Investigates furtively

Puzzle 3
a. Halts
b. Notices something

Puzzle 4
a. Unappealing features or qualities
b. Dried cereal stalks

Image Combination

Imagine combining these two images, so each white square in one is filled with the contents of the corresponding square in the other image. How many stars would there be in total?

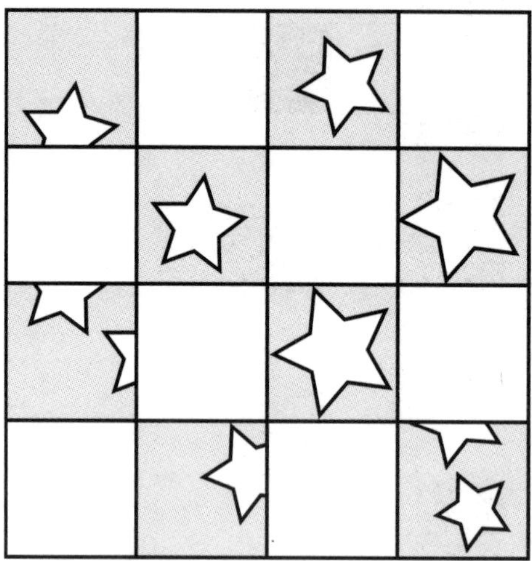

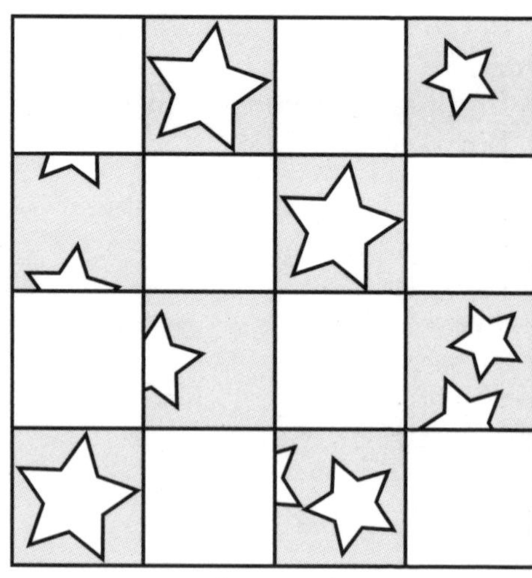

Mini Crossword

Solve each of the clues to complete this mini-crossword grid.

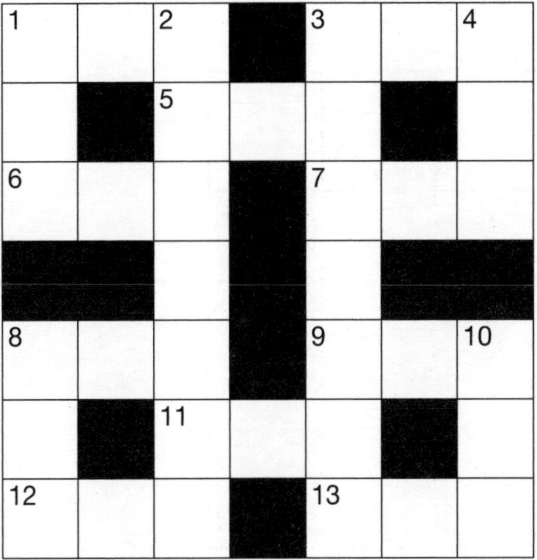

Across

1 Amateur radio operator (3)
3 Golfing average (3)
5 Intense temper (3)
6 Pimple-inducing viral disease (3)
7 Hogwash (3)
8 Greek 'T' (3)
9 Tea dispenser (3)
11 Hydraulic lifting machine (3)
12 Expression of mild sympathy (3)
13 Piece of corn (3)

Down

1 Joint between the thigh and pelvis (3)
2 Combination (7)
3 Fragrance (7)
4 Large, mouse-like rodent (3)
8 Duvet unit (3)
10 'Neither' correlative (3)

Futoshiki

Place 1 to 5 once each in every row and column, while obeying the greater-than signs – if there is a sign between two squares, then the arrow always points at the smaller of the two numbers.

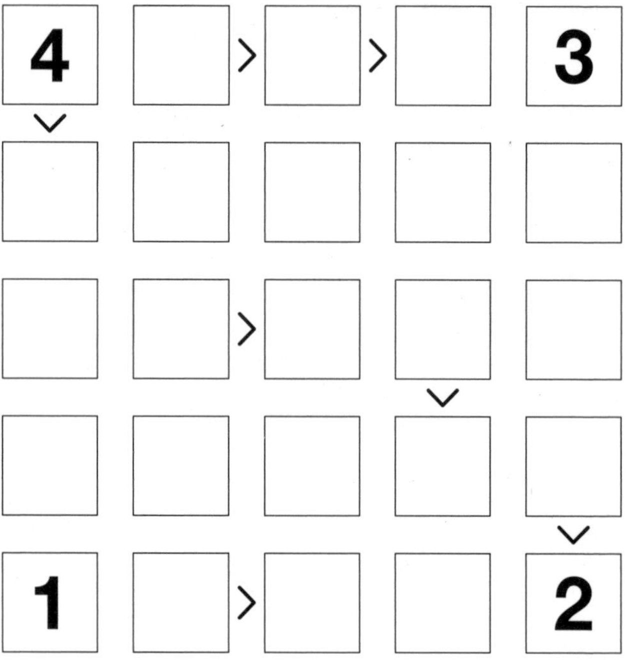

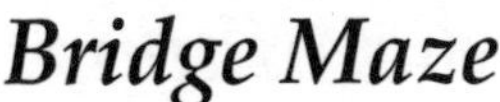

Bridge Maze

Can you find your way through this maze, travelling from the entrance at the top all the way down to the exit at the bottom? The maze contains a number of bridges, which allow you to pass either over or under a path – but not to move between crossing paths.

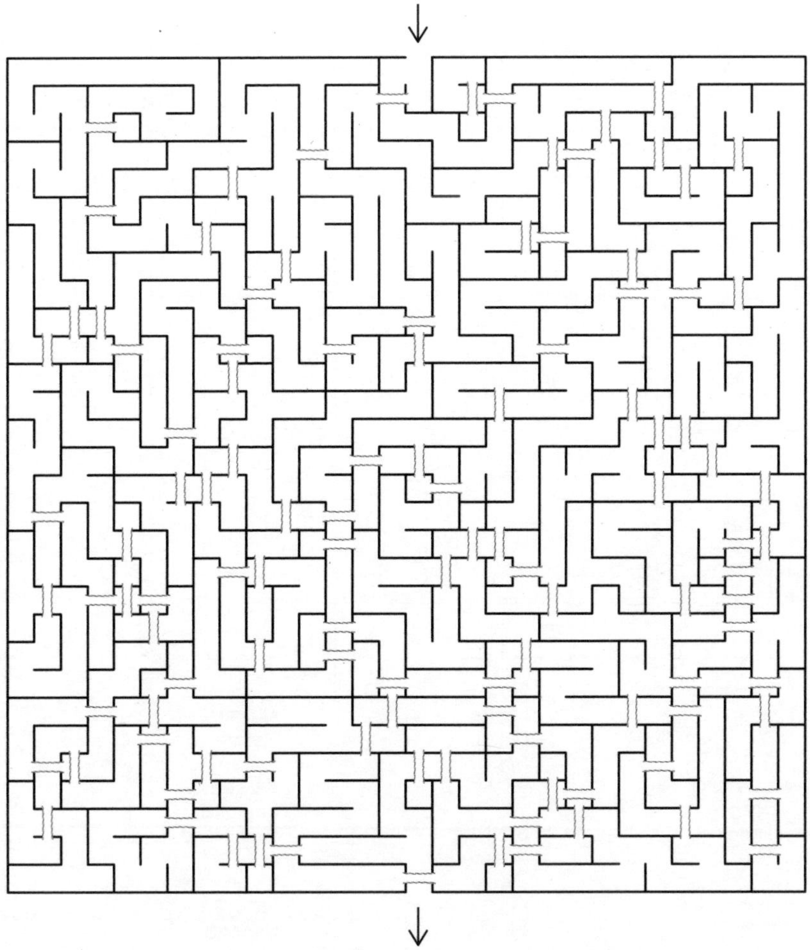

↓

↓

Word Placement

Fit all the listed words into the grid, crossword-style.

3 Letters
Nee
Wet

4 Letters
Does
Twee

5 Letters
Aside
Darts
Eased
Evens
Islet
Lithe
Meets
Rinse
Salsa
Vital

6 Letters
Deemed
Eldest
Placed
Studio

7 Letters
Concern
Moments
Nirvana
Rotated

9 Letters
Interpret
Reminisce

11 Letters
Arrangement
Bridegrooms

Spot the Changes

First, cover up the bottom of the page (below the dividing line), then spend up to a minute remembering the list of fruit, then cover it over, wait a few seconds, and then see if you can spot which ones have been replaced on the copy of the list at the bottom of the page.

Kumquat	Pineapple	Strawberry
Watermelon	Grape	Elderberry
Banana	Orange	Kiwi
Nectarine	Apple	Raspberry
Peach	Satsuma	Cherry

Kumquat	Pineapple	Blackberry
Pomegranate	Grape	Elderberry
Lychee	Orange	Clementine
Nectarine	Apple	Lemon
Pear	Lime	Cherry

Dot Drawing

Try this creative task by drawing straight lines to join some, or all, of the dots together. See if you can come up with a pattern or picture, just with this restricted set of dots. Even if you have no idea what you want to draw, just start by joining dots at random and see what it begins to look like!

Arrow Word

All of this crossword's clues are given inside the grid.

Be in the red		Elongated fish		Archaic		Type of ski race		Tea, orange ___
Greets								
				Spy		No longer batting?		Letter following chi
Undesirable plant	Bushy hairdo (abbr)		Receiver					
Ford van		Full of anxiety		Shades				
							Time without war	
Repeatedly				Ballpoint, eg		Camera opening		Pelted along
Flying vehicle	Responds							
					Knock on a door			
'Candy Crush' sequel suffix	Small hotel				Barman's query			
				Took advantage of				

Solutions

Page 9

E	C	O	A	I	R	G	P	M	U	A	G	F	A	A
Z	A	L	A	I	A	O	A	R	M	G	L	A	A	R
L	P	A	R	G	L	R	S	A	N	Y	C	W	G	O
G	A	I	C	E	O	O	R	E	P	D	A	A	C	I
F	R	Z	L	D	W	Y	N	P	A	R	L	B	A	S
E	P	L	A	U	L	O	O	G	E	I	I	T	U	A
A	G	H	A	L	T	P	L	I	A	C	L	L	H	Y
A	A	D	I	R	E	I	A	F	A	M	O	B	Y	D
R	L	S	I	P	E	A	D	R	N	I	N	E	D	A
I	W	E	C	H	O	B	N	T	D	U	O	G	R	F
S	T	I	I	G	C	A	R	A	M	A	S	O	A	F
O	L	A	R	D	T	R	L	E	N	F	F	N	N	O
R	E	D	R	I	A	G	O	D	G	I	H	I	G	D
E	I	I	O	A	I	S	E	E	R	F	P	A	E	I
A	A	N	G	R	O	C	I	A	R	A	L	P	A	L

Page 11

Crafts: spacecrafts / craftsman
Tread: sightread / treadmill
Hand: freehand / handcuffed

Page 12

Page 13

Composure uses all the letters.

Other words include come, comer, comers, comes, compose, composer, coo, coop, cooper, coopers, coops, coos, cop, cope, copes, cops, copse, core, cores, corm, corms, corps, corpse, corpus, coup, coupe, coupes, coups, course, crop, crops, croup, croups, cue, cues, cup, cups, cur, cure, cures, curs, curse, cusp, ecru, recoup, recoups, scoop, scope, score, scour, scum, source, spec and spruce

Page 14

1 + 57 = 58	43 + 17 = 60
29 - 1 = 28	11 + 42 = 53
10 × 5 = 50	12 + 11 = 23
71 + 20 = 91	24 - 12 = 12
5 ÷ 5 = 1	14 ÷ 7 = 2
5 × 9 = 45	10 × 9 = 90
12 × 4 = 48	15 ÷ 3 = 5
2 + 67 = 69	7 + 54 = 61
48 - 5 = 43	11 × 7 = 77
30 ÷ 6 = 5	44 - 8 = 36

Page 15

Aqua, septets, amoeba, neuron gulag, encase, saws

Solutions

Page 17

T	U	E	H	S	C	N	N	S	L	C	E	U	S	B
L	L	R	S	N	E	E	E	A	H	R	E	T	M	U
U	L	A	F	S	E	R	R	S	E	W	E	C	H	R
B	R	E	S	G	N	A	F	B	S	L	S	H	E	H
G	N	O	H	I	B	W	M	N	B	V	N	U	L	S
H	M	F	S	U	N	I	E	A	C	M	R	E	N	R
U	T	E	S	R	L	R	T	A	R	F	P	E	R	N
S	R	H	E	C	M	E	C	O	A	E	E	E	E	I
B	E	F	L	B	G	T	I	R	R	R	E	N	W	L
L	C	A	E	E	U	L	S	E	G	R	U	I	O	V
D	E	I	V	S	I	B	N	R	C	D	U	V	L	R
B	R	E	F	C	N	N	E	U	L	E	R	T	F	I
R	B	C	H	S	I	V	T	R	E	E	S	R	G	L
R	E	E	E	A	E	E	V	S	R	W	H	E	R	B
W	N	S	L	T	I	L	E	S	C	E	A	L	R	W

Page 18

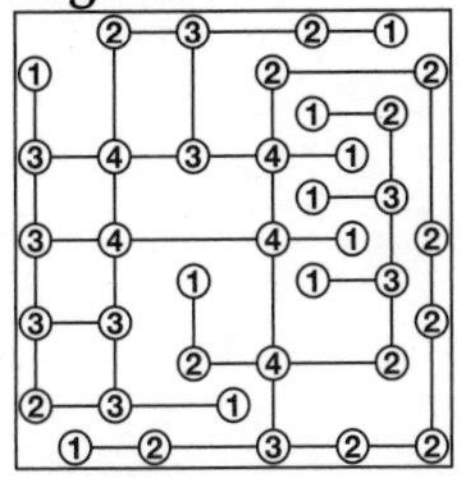

Page 19

4	2	3	1
1	3	2	4
2	4	1	3
3	1	4	2

2	4	3	1
3	1	4	2
4	2	1	3
1	3	2	4

3	4	2	1
2	1	3	4
1	3	4	2
4	2	1	3

3	4	2	1
1	2	4	3
4	3	1	2
2	1	3	4

Page 20

39	13	4	2	3	**22**
80	41	118	59	29	**46**
489	619	442	34	500	**300**

Page 21

Sideboard, wardrobe, curtain, cabinet, footstool

Page 22

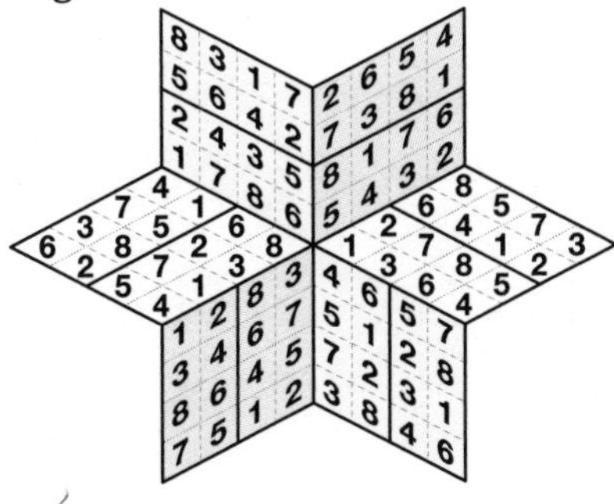

Page 23

1	6	3	7	5	4	2
3	4	1	5	7	2	6
7	5	2	3	4	6	1
6	1	5	2	3	7	4
4	2	7	6	1	3	5
2	7	4	1	6	5	3
5	3	6	4	2	1	7

Page 24

Earmuff, washroom, aerobics, mushroom, kangaroo

Page 25

A		I		S				A		A		T
D	O	N	A	T	E	S		L	U	N	C	H
V		F		R		E		L		T		U
A	G	O		O	B	T	A	I	N	I	N	G
N				K		T		E		D		
C	Y	C	L	E		L	E	S	S	O	N	S
E		R				E				T		U
D	I	A	G	R	A	M		C	R	E	E	P
		Y		A		E		H				P
R	E	F	E	R	E	N	C	E		G	O	O
O		I		E		T		Q		I		S
L	I	S	T	S		S	H	U	F	F	L	E
E		H		T				E		T		D

Solutions

Page 27

12 × 9 =	108	9 × 6 =	54
12 × 16 =	192	84 ÷ 7 =	12
14 + 92 =	106	76 + 19 =	95
26 + 91 =	117	9 × 14 =	126
9 × 5 =	45	182÷ 7 =	26
9 × 15 =	135	41 + 9 =	50
13 × 2 =	26	30 - 25 =	5
43 - 29 =	14	11 × 5 =	55
49 - 29 =	20	18 + 18 =	36
8 × 6 =	48	10 - 6 =	4

Page 28

	G		I		B		A	
	I		N		I	S	L	E
A	B	S	T	R	A	C	T	
	B	E	E		S	H	E	D
	E	A	R	N		O	R	E
	R		N			O	N	E
H	I	M		S		L	A	D
	S	O	B	E	R		T	
	H	U	R	T		D	I	D
		N	I	T		I	V	Y
V	E	T	O		K	N	E	E

Page 29

Bagpipes, accordion, glockenspiel, saxophone, recorder

Page 30

Emotional uses all the letters. Other words include aloe, alone, alto, atom, atone, elation, emotion, eon, into, ion, iota, lemon, lion, loam, loan, loin, lone, loom, loon, loot, lot, lotion, melon, moan, moat, mole, molten, moo, moon, moot, mote, motel, motile, motion, noel, not, note, oaten, oil, oleo, omen, omit, one, onto, talon, toe, toenail, toil, tom, tome, ton, tonal, tone, too and tool

Page 33

Page 34

2	●	●		2	●
2	●	4	3	●	2
	4	●			1
●	4	●	4	2	
2		●	●	2	●
1	●		2	2	1

Page 35

Tests, hidden, trivia, wonders

Page 36

D	E	N	I	Z	E	N
I	■	A	■	A	■	O
S	K	I	■	P	R	O
P	■	L	O	P	■	D
U	N	I	■	I	L	L
T	■	N	■	N	■	E
E	N	G	A	G	E	S

Solutions

Page 37

Words include mess, mete, mons, moss, most, mote, mots, muse, muss, must, mute, mutt, nene, ness, nest, nets, nett, none, nose, note, nuns, nuts, pens, pent, pest, pets, pone, pons, pont, pose, poss, post, pots, puns, punt, puss, puts and putt

Page 38

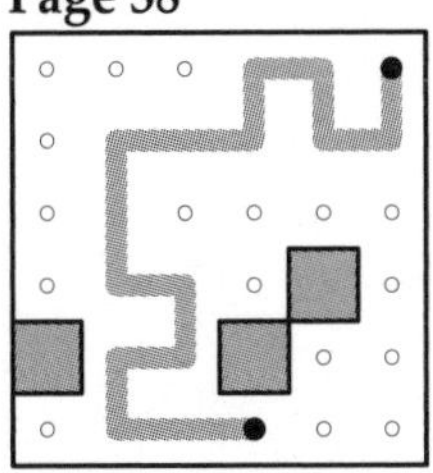

Page 40

Library, conservatory, kitchen, basement, bathroom

Page 42

R	M	D	S	S	U	D	O	K	U	R	S	N	G	F
S	U	E	I	I	E	C	A	O	E	G	U	O	U	E
R	E	O	O	O	M	C	R	C	K	M	L	T	I	S
E	G	O	C	A	R	P	T	O	B	A	O	E	N	O
D	L	U	N	E	S	A	L	E	S	S	K	O	A	R
D	H	N	S	I	N	S	R	E	H	S	H	U	E	L
A	G	C	H	G	M	L	S	I	L	R	W	R	R	A
L	W	R	L	S	I	O	K	A	M	O	O	O	O	O
D	S	E	S	N	H	I	D	O	O	S	O	N	R	I
R	S	S	K	D	R	O	W	T	I	F	S	P	M	D
O	E	N	E	A	D	A	R	R	O	W	W	O	R	D
W	Z	O	R	H	C	R	A	E	S	D	R	O	W	G
E	A	W	G	K	B	R	I	D	G	E	S	E	E	O
A	M	A	N	A	G	R	A	M	S	L	R	R	I	S
S	L	I	T	H	E	R	L	I	N	K	L	F	O	D

Page 43

100 ÷ 5 =	20	74 - 21 =	53
52 - 24 =	28	97 + 7 =	104
15 + 23 =	38	78 - 15 =	63
23 + 92 =	115	8 × 12 =	96
29 - 23 =	6	10 + 56 =	66
8 - 7 =	1	16 - 12 =	4
56 + 6 =	62	6 × 3 =	18
58 ÷ 2 =	29	62 - 9 =	53
92 - 10 =	82	114 ÷ 2 =	57
125 ÷ 5 =	25	41 + 9 =	50

Page 44

Possible words include fleer, flees, floes, floss, flues, flump, freer, frees, froes, frump, sleep, sloes, slues, slump, slums, steep, steer, stems, stoep, stomp, stump, stums, trees, tress, tromp, truer, trues, trump and truss

Page 45

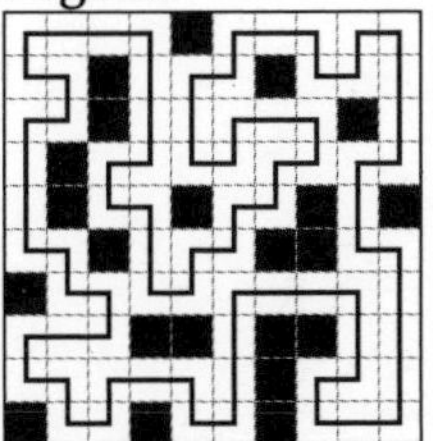

Page 46

81 = 37 + 23 + 21
82 = 14 + 39 + 29
83 = 32 + 22 + 29

Solutions

Page 47

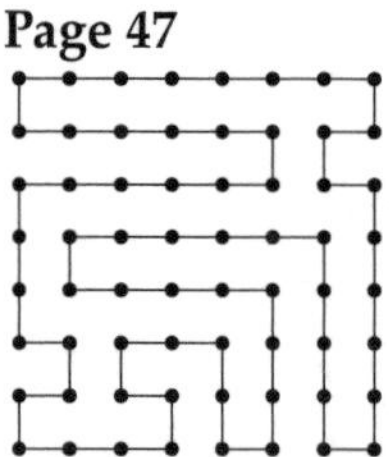

Page 48

COME › CAME › CASE › BASE › BASK › BACK

Page 49

Ports	Strop
Paws	Swap
Golf	Flog
Remit	Timer

Page 50

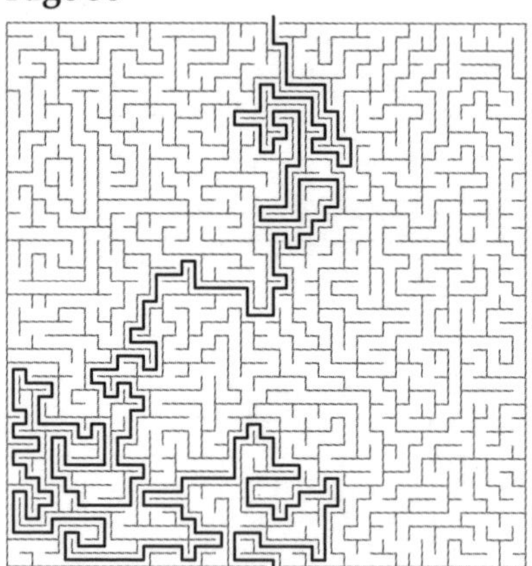

Page 51

Sleep: oversleep / sleepless
Post: signpost / postage
Bread: cornbread / breadwinner

Page 52

Incomprehensible uses all the letters. Other words include bin, comb, comprehensible, core, hen, hens, her, hero, ibis, isle, lei, more, nib, ore, pie, pis, pro, prom, romp and sip

Page 54

B	E	D	C	A
E	C	A	D	B
A	D	E	B	C
D	B	C	A	E
C	A	B	E	D

D	C	A	E	B
C	B	E	D	A
E	A	C	B	D
B	E	D	A	C
A	D	B	C	E

Page 55

Phased	Shaped
Pierce	Recipe
Player	Replay
Poster	Presto
Priest	Stripe
Primes	Simper
Pseudo	Souped
Reigns	Singer
Resets	Steers
Resist	Sister
Rising	Siring
Rivets	Strive
Rushes	Ushers
Sadden	Sanded
Sheets	Theses

Solutions

Page 56

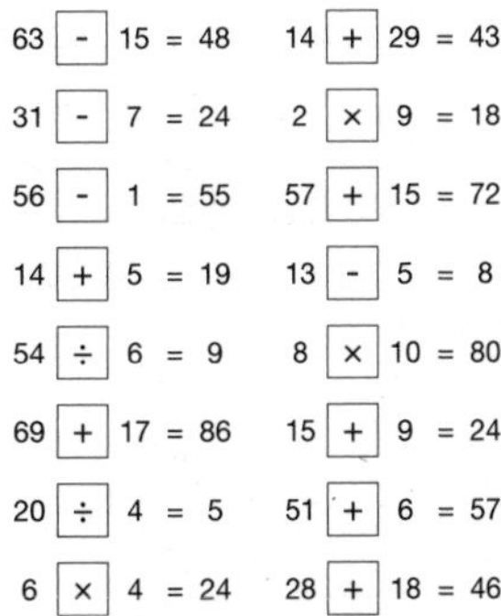

63 - 15 = 48   14 + 29 = 43
31 - 7 = 24   2 × 9 = 18
56 - 1 = 55   57 + 15 = 72
14 + 5 = 19   13 - 5 = 8
54 ÷ 6 = 9   8 × 10 = 80
69 + 17 = 86   15 + 9 = 24
20 ÷ 4 = 5   51 + 6 = 57
6 × 4 = 24   28 + 18 = 46
31 + 11 = 42   144 ÷ 12 = 12
18 + 2 = 20   74 + 14 = 88

Page 57

B	O	A	R			
	R		E	O	N	
	P		A		E	
S	H	A	D	O	W	S
	A		I		E	
	N	I	L		S	
			Y	E	T	I

Page 58

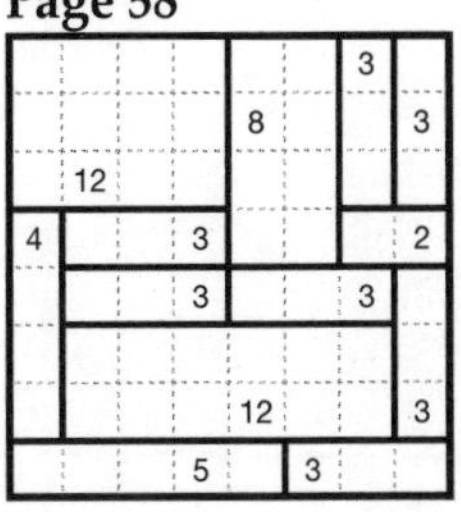

Page 59

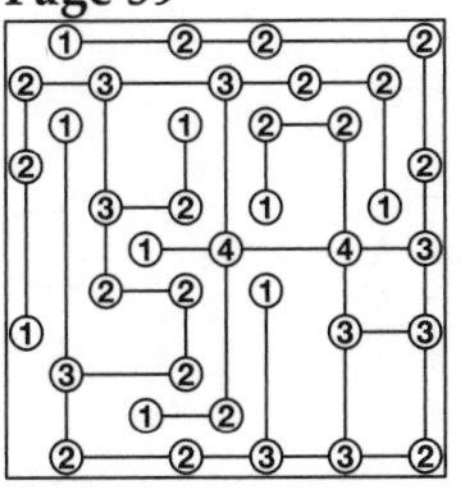

Page 60

U	N	C	L	E	A	R		S	P	A	S	M
	E		E		M		V		H		E	
P	S	Y	C	H	O	L	O	G	I	C	A	L
	T		T		N		O				S	
D	E	B	U	G	G	E	D		T	O	O	K
	D		R				O		R		N	
		F	I	C	T	I	O	N	A	L		
	P		N		E				N		I	
S	O	N	G		C	R	O	S	S	I	N	G
	U				H		P		P		V	
I	N	T	E	R	N	A	T	I	O	N	A	L
	D		G		O		I		R		D	
U	S	A	G	E		S	C	A	T	T	E	R

Page 61

Twilit, chic, seers, trait, cleric, salvos, blab

Page 62

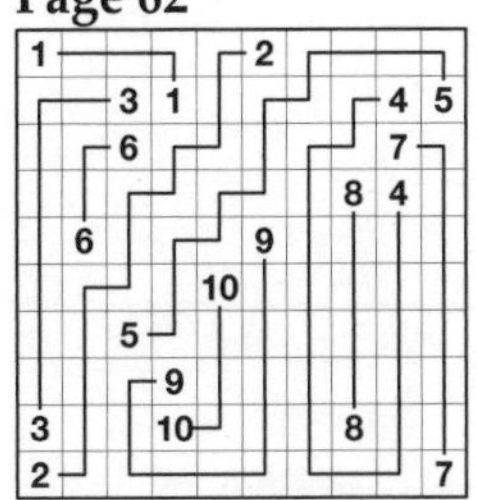

Solutions

Page 63

19:55 + 01:40 = **21:35**

14:00 + 05:55 = **19:55**

13:35 - 08:45 = **04:50**

18:05 + 04:55 = **23:00**

06:45 + 10:45 = **17:30**

11:50 + 05:35 = **17:25**

05:45 - 04:15 = **01:30**

18:45 - 13:45 = **05:00**

04:15 + 05:00 = **09:15**

11:05 + 06:45 = **17:50**

Page 64

E	C	B	D	A	F
D	A	F	E	C	B
F	E	C	B	D	A
B	D	A	F	E	C
A	F	E	C	B	D
C	B	D	A	F	E

Page 65

2	5	1 <	3	4
3	2	4	1	5
		v		
4	3	2	5	1
	^	^		^
1	4	5	2	3
5	1	3	4 >	2

Page 66

Snooker
Volleyball
Golf
Lacrosse
Rugby
Basketball
Skiing
Baseball
Gliding
Karate
Judo
Handball
Football
Windsurfing
Cricket
Hockey

Page 67

Page 68

5	17	13	31	16	**24**
40	160	16	88	44	**33**
221	395	474	451	205	**306**

Page 69

E	L	P	R	R	R	R	L	L	P	O	R	L	E	P
L	S	P	L	E	E	A	R	K	I	E	E	R	R	O
N	G	H	I	L	V	A	A	G	I	L	I	I	O	A
M	R	Z	G	N	P	E	R	R	L	P	R	S	D	Z
K	K	A	Z	O	S	D	I	E	U	D	R	S	A	E
P	E	E	O	T	C	C	S	R	N	N	E	L	R	L
B	N	D	L	O	I	S	H	U	T	K	T	I	B	N
P	L	H	L	P	U	P	H	E	L	E	D	K	A	I
E	A	L	U	R	I	S	S	E	R	H	R	O	L	T
N	I	P	K	S	H	E	K	E	P	E	L	E	A	N
E	I	C	O	C	K	E	R	S	P	A	N	I	E	L
L	A	A	A	L	L	Y	E	A	I	T	O	O	R	O
J	E	D	A	D	A	L	M	A	T	I	A	N	Z	E
T	D	A	S	P	S	H	E	E	P	D	O	G	E	H
A	R	E	Z	U	A	N	H	C	S	I	E	O	D	E

Solutions

Page 70

1	0	2	2	3	2	4	3
0	4	5	6	3	5	5	1
0	0	6	4	4	2	4	0
5	2	6	0	4	2	3	3
0	2	4	6	2	6	1	1
5	1	3	5	5	5	1	1
1	6	6	3	3	0	4	6

Page 71

0	0	1	0	1	1	0	1
0	0	1	0	1	0	1	1
1	1	0	1	0	1	0	0
1	0	0	1	1	0	0	1
0	1	1	0	0	1	1	0
0	0	1	0	1	0	1	1
1	1	0	1	0	1	0	0
1	1	0	1	0	0	1	0

Page 73

	S		P		C		D	
	A		A		A	B	E	T
S	M	O	G		Y	E	P	
	U	D	O	N		F	L	U
	R	E	D		C	O	O	S
	A		A			R	Y	E
D	I	G		B	Y	E		
		U		O		H	I	T
W	O	M	A	N		A	D	O
	V		G	U	I	N	E	A
W	A	G	E	S		D	A	D

Page 74

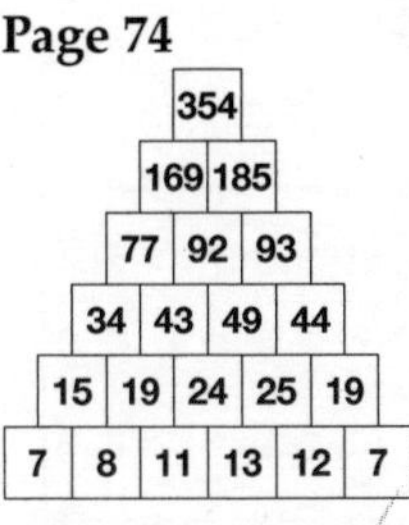

Page 75

Cappuccino, macchiato, espresso, americano, filter

Page 76

7	6	5	4	1	2	3
6	2	1	5	4	3	7
1	3	4	6	2	7	5
2	5	6	7	3	4	1
4	7	2	3	5	1	6
5	4	3	1	7	6	2
3	1	7	2	6	5	4

Page 77

36 cubes: 3 on the top level, 5 on the second level, 10 on the third level and 18 on the bottom level

Page 78

Page 79

DAFT › DART › PART › PORT › POET › POEM

Page 80

Comfortable, unhurried, leisurely, unconcerned, carefree

Solutions

Page 81

Page 82

LOVE 〉 LONE 〉 TONE 〉 TONS 〉 TENS 〉 TEAS

Page 83

4	2	3	1
1	3	2	4
2	1	4	3
3	4	1	2

3	2	1	4
1	4	3	2
4	3	2	1
2	1	4	3

4	3	2	1
2	1	4	3
3	4	1	2
1	2	3	4

4	1	2	3
3	2	1	4
2	3	4	1
1	4	3	2

Page 84

Purple, aquamarine, chocolate, magnolia, lavender

Page 85

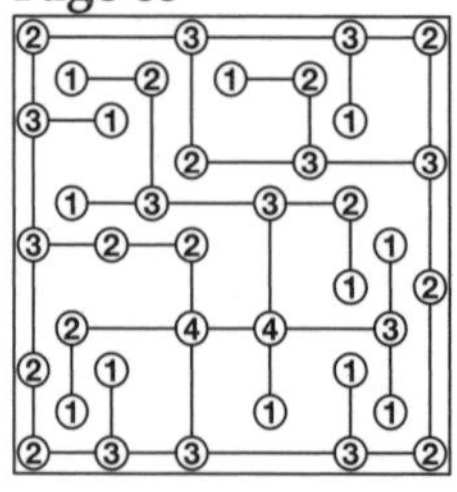

Page 86

	P		V		C		B		F		A	
S	A	L	A	M	I		O	N	L	I	N	E
	R		M		C		N		A		G	
S	K	I	P		A	S	S	E	M	B	L	E
	I				D		A		B		E	
I	N	I	T	I	A	L	I	Z	E	D		
	G		H						A		R	
		C	O	N	S	T	I	T	U	T	E	D
	M		R		A		G				A	
L	O	C	A	T	I	O	N		R	I	L	E
	O		C		L		O		U		I	
A	D	V	I	C	E		R	O	B	O	T	S
	Y		C		D		E		S		Y	

Page 88

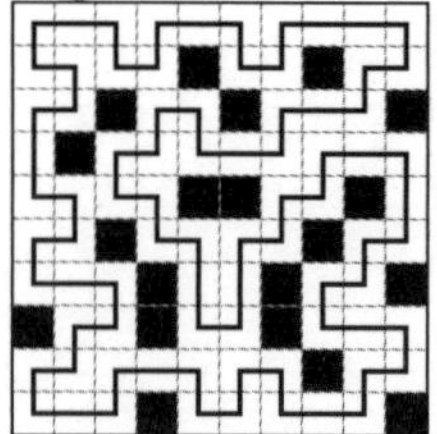

Page 89

	R	U	B	B	E	R
	I		E			U
I	S	O	L	A	T	E
	K				R	
D	Y	N	A	M	I	C
O			H		C	
E	M	B	A	R	K	

Page 90

Transcendentally uses all the letters. Other words include all, ally, art, cent, dell, den, dent, dental, ell, end, led, lent, let, natal, net, ran, rat, scent, scented, tall, tally, tan, tans, tar, tars, tart,

Solutions

tell, ten, tent, transcend and transcendent

Page 91

Angers Ranges
Ardent Ranted
Armpit Impart
Ashore Hoarse
Aspire Praise
Assent Sanest
Belied Edible
Bosses Obsess
Caress Scares
Cedars Sacred
Creams Scream
Decals Scaled
Decors Scored
Denial Nailed
Deport Ported

Page 92

Mood Doom
Loots Stool
Denier Reined
Devil Lived

Page 93

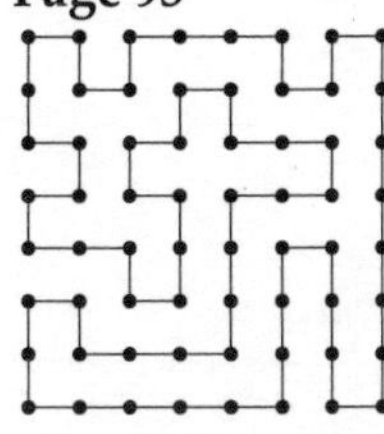

Page 94

O	X	D	N	O	M	A	I	D	E	S	R	S	E	A
N	I	C	D	E	A	E	D	L	G	Q	I	U	S	R
M	R	R	O	H	S	H	S	T	O	U	P	B	P	E
A	N	A	M	N	L	C	T	G	P	A	R	M	I	E
R	C	E	T	G	O	L	O	R	H	R	L	O	L	H
G	E	E	C	S	P	G	E	N	I	E	R	H	L	O
O	L	N	A	N	E	Y	A	I	E	A	L	R	E	N
L	T	D	P	E	I	L	R	X	T	L	N	S	O	T
E	N	L	L	E	S	N	G	A	E	L	R	G	R	A
L	C	A	L	R	N	P	E	N	M	H	A	I	L	T
L	A	V	U	G	R	T	H	L	A	I	A	O	D	E
A	N	O	O	H	Y	S	A	E	C	T	D	T	L	O
R	O	M	T	T	R	C	Q	G	R	R	C	C	L	N
A	S	O	C	T	A	G	O	N	O	E	I	E	A	R
P	D	P	N	A	L	R	E	A	S	N	O	C	R	L

Page 96

359
160 199
71 89 110
34 37 52 58
19 15 22 30 28
11 8 7 15 15 13

Page 97

Ward: eastward / wardrobe
Walk: catwalk / walkout
Where: everywhere / whereupon

Page 99

	D		D		S		B	
	E		I		U	N	I	T
E	G	G	S		M	O	O	
	R	A	C	K		T		A
	E	G	O		G	I	R	L
B	E	A	U	T	I	F	U	L
	S		R		G	Y	M	
		O	A	R				I
S	U	G	G	E	S	T	E	D
		L	E	D		A	W	E
P	R	E	S	S	U	R	E	S

Solutions

Page 100

9	3	6	31	23	**44**
84	21	95	190	103	**181**
259	148	222	74	518	**392**

Page 101

Possible words include dame, dams, dans, date, dens, dime, dims, dine, dins, dits, dune, duns, rams, rate, rats, rete, rets, rime, rims, rine, rite, rums, rune, runs, ruts, tame, tams, tans, tats, tens, tete, time, tine, tins, tits, tums, tune, tuns and tuts

Page 102

Dreamer (or dreamier), quarrel, mindful, wonderful and awesomeness

Page 103

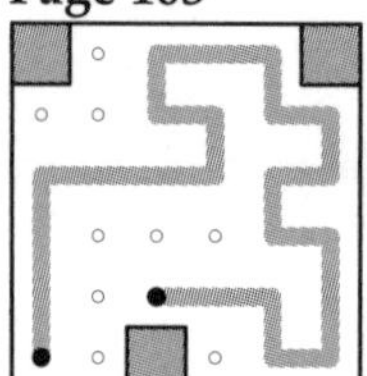

Page 104

0	0	1	0	1	0	1	1
1	0	0	1	1	0	0	1
0	1	1	0	0	1	1	0
0	0	1	0	1	1	0	1
1	1	0	1	0	0	1	0
0	0	1	0	1	1	0	1
1	1	0	1	0	1	0	0
1	1	0	1	0	0	1	0

Page 106

Quietness uses all the letters. Other words include ensue, ensues, equine, equines, inquest, inquests, issue, nut, nuts, queen, quest, quests, quiet, quiets, quit, quite, quits, sequin, sequins, sinus, squint, squints, stun, stuns, sue, sues, suet, suit, suite, suites, suits, sun, suns, sunset, tissue, tun, tune, tunes, tuns, unit, unite, unites, units, unset, untie, unties, use and uses

Page 107

$1 + 21 = 22$	$17 - 2 = 15$
$2 + 16 = 18$	$36 \div 12 = 3$
$2 + 17 = 19$	$59 - 13 = 46$
$12 \times 12 = 144$	$73 + 8 = 81$
$7 + 17 = 24$	$14 + 10 = 24$
$44 + 19 = 63$	$15 + 62 = 77$
$7 + 12 = 19$	$40 \div 8 = 5$
$33 - 4 = 29$	$132 \div 11 = 12$
$23 - 10 = 13$	$3 \times 9 = 27$
$3 \times 5 = 15$	$36 - 2 = 34$

Page 109

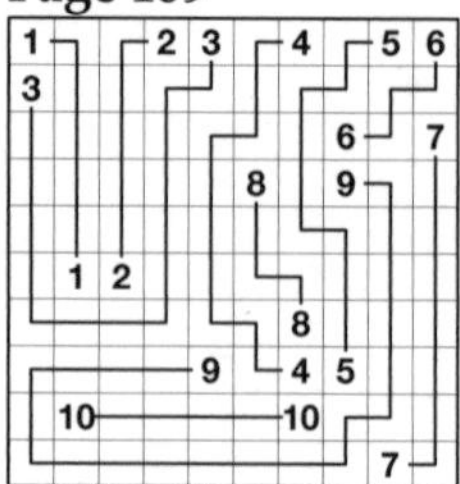

Solutions

Page 110

1	3 ‹	4 ‹	5	2
2 ^	4	1 ^	3	5
5	2	3	4	1
3	5	2	1	4 v
4	1	5	2 ‹	3

Page 112

Courgette, beetroot, onion, sweetcorn, celery, asparagus

Page 113

D	C	B	E	A
B	A	E	C	D
C	E	D	A	B
E	B	A	D	C
A	D	C	B	E

D	A	C	E	B
A	B	E	D	C
E	C	D	B	A
B	E	A	C	D
C	D	B	A	E

Page 114

■	C	L	I	M	B	S
■	O	■	M	■	O	■
S	C	R	I	P	T	■
■	H	■	T	■	T	■
■	L	I	A	B	L	E
■	E	■	T	■	E	■
L	A	B	E	L	S	■

Page 115

32 - 22 =	10	28 + 24 =	52
12 × 11 =	132	36 + 20 =	56
26 - 9 =	17	4 × 8 =	32
17 + 86 =	103	31 - 8 =	23
10 + 55 =	65	12 + 23 =	35
28 - 10 =	18	189 ÷ 3 =	63
5 × 15 =	75	10 + 6 =	16
192 ÷ 12 =	16	10 × 4 =	40
65 - 6 =	59	96 - 25 =	71
84 - 10 =	74	27 + 27 =	54

Page 116

Deckchair, sunglasses, swimsuit, snorkel, surfboard

Page 117

Silhouette C

Page 118

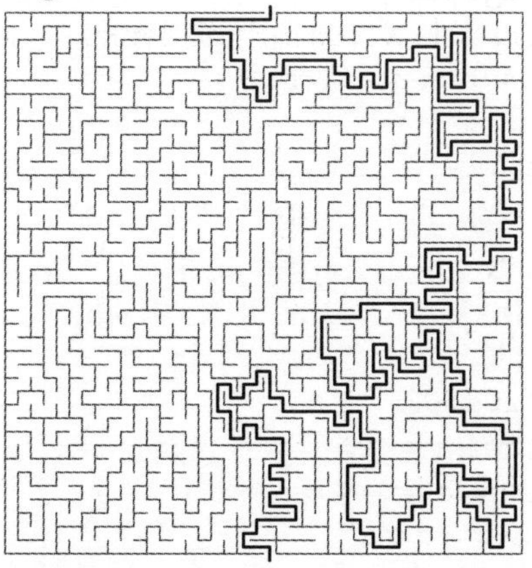

Page 119

Torrent, swards, daybed, topcoat, armada, cynic, haunch

Page 120

There are 7 circles:

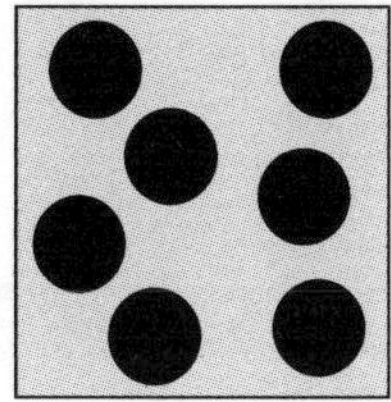

Solutions

Page 121

	D		S		S		I	
	E		A		U	R	N	S
D	E	C	L	A	R	E	S	
	P	E	A		F	A	T	E
	E	N	D			C	R	Y
A	R	T		E		H	U	E
		U	G	L	Y		C	
		R	E	F		A	T	E
C	H	I	C		S	L	I	M
		E	K	E		G	N	U
A	L	S	O		T	A	G	S

Page 122

32 cubes: 3 on the top level, 5 on the second level, 10 on the third level and 14 on the bottom level

Page 123

I	E	M	S	M	O	F	S	I	G	N	I	P	L	A
A	O	R	I	E	Y	T	L	A	Y	O	L	I	O	I
I	A	B	B	C	N	G	I	S	M	S	C	N	D	L
S	T	R	A	A	R	I	Y	E	I	O	E	A	N	E
A	U	I	I	E	I	O	P	I	W	C	A	I	A	O
I	V	T	S	I	N	S	N	P	G	A	G	I	I	R
I	A	I	E	E	A	A	E	E	I	N	C	A	N	I
N	L	S	N	A	O	C	E	N	S	L	S	W	O	A
L	U	H	Y	I	O	S	I	G	A	I	I	A	I	B
U	I	V	L	C	I	E	G	R	E	L	A	H	R	S
A	R	I	O	Y	R	I	P	I	A	A	E	E	P	I
T	A	R	P	I	A	I	T	N	J	E	M	M	O	F
I	A	G	D	R	A	W	E	E	L	I	L	M	N	I
I	E	I	E	E	N	A	E	A	G	F	F	A	M	L
C	A	N	A	R	Y	A	E	O	L	I	A	N	B	U

Page 124

	O	S	T	R	I	C	H		Q	U	I	T
S		T		E		R				P		E
C	H	E	A	P	L	Y		C	A	S	T	S
R		E		E		I		H		I		T
A	D	D	E	R		N	O	O	D	L	E	
T				T		G		L		O		S
C	A	R	B	O	N		H	E	R	N	I	A
H		E		I		S		S				U
	C	L	E	R	G	Y		T	A	S	K	S
U		Y		E		S		E		P		A
S	W	I	M	S		T	U	R	N	I	N	G
E		N				E		O		K		E
S	I	G	H		I	M	P	L	I	E	D	

Page 125

Words include leaks, leeks, loner, peace, peaks, peeks, pence, ponce, prees, reeks and rones

Page 127

F	C	B	D	E	A
B	E	F	A	C	D
A	D	C	E	F	B
E	F	A	B	D	C
D	B	E	C	A	F
C	A	D	F	B	E

Page 128

●	1		●	●	1
2		3	●	4	
●	3	●	3	●	2
●	5		3	2	●
●	4	●			1
1		●	●	1	

Page 131

Word, puppy, bonus, climate

Solutions

Page 132

Photographically uses all the letters. Other words include all, ally, argot, art, call, got, graph, graphic, graphical, graphically, hall, hot, oar, par, part, photo, photograph, photographic, rap, toy and trap

Page 133

22:35 - 18:20 =	**04:15**
23:40 - 21:50 =	**01:50**
07:25 + 06:05 =	**13:30**
11:00 + 06:10 =	**17:10**
13:20 - 05:15 =	**08:05**
09:55 + 04:20 =	**14:15**
02:25 - 01:10 =	**01:15**
21:50 - 03:50 =	**18:00**
09:35 + 07:40 =	**17:15**
12:40 + 09:15 =	**21:55**

Page 134

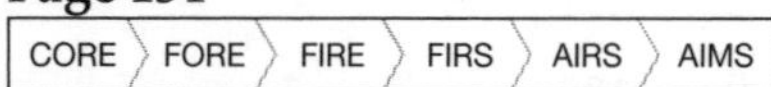

Page 136

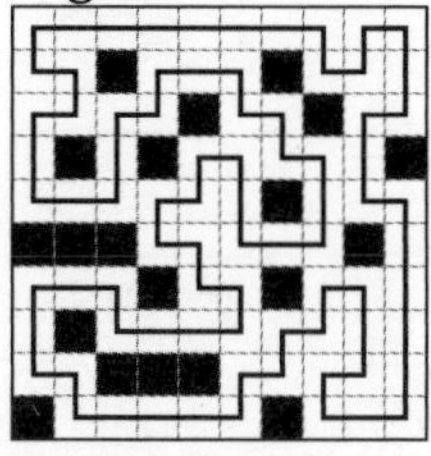

Page 137

Attention uses all the letters. Other words include anion, anoint, anon, ant, ante, anti, atone, eon, inane, inn, innate, intent, into, intone, ion, nation, neat, neon, net, nine, nit, none, not, note, oaten, one, taint, tan, ten, tenant, tenon, tent, tin, tine, tint, titan, ton, tone and tonne

Page 138

27	+	5	=	32		4	×	12	=	48
60	÷	10	=	6		28	+	4	=	32
28	-	3	=	25		63	-	11	=	52
24	÷	6	=	4		2	×	10	=	20
49	÷	7	=	7		72	÷	12	=	6
3	×	4	=	12		3	×	5	=	15
7	+	4	=	11		12	+	15	=	27
6	×	6	=	36		41	-	11	=	30
7	×	5	=	35		62	-	6	=	56
17	+	69	=	86		7	×	8	=	56

Page 139

B		O		D		S		G		F		A
A	M	U	S	E		P	U	L	L	I	N	G
L		T		L		O		A		R		E
S	I	L	L	I	E	R		D	E	M	O	N
A		I				T		I				D
M	A	N	I	F	E	S	T	O		V	I	A
		E		L				L		E		
D	U	D		A	B	O	L	I	S	H	E	S
E				B		D				I		A
T	H	R	O	B		D	E	F	I	C	I	T
E		E		I		I		E		L		I
S	C	A	R	L	E	T		T	H	E	I	R
T		R		Y		Y		E		S		E

Page 140

Hydrogen, oxygen, krypton, chlorine, neon

Solutions

Page 141

Page 142

S	P	I	D	E	R	■
■	I	■	I	■	O	■
P	R	E	M	I	U	M
■	A	■	■	■	G	■
G	N	O	C	C	H	I
■	H	■	A	■	L	■
■	A	R	R	A	Y	S

Page 143

84 - 25 =	**59**	23 + 99 =	**122**
171 ÷ 9 =	**19**	46 - 22 =	**24**
51 - 19 =	**32**	7 × 5 =	**35**
67 - 12 =	**55**	136 ÷ 2 =	**68**
3 × 4 =	**12**	22 + 77 =	**99**
10 × 18 =	**180**	8 + 90 =	**98**
17 + 48 =	**65**	84 - 29 =	**55**
73 - 28 =	**45**	22 + 73 =	**95**
192 ÷ 3 =	**64**	13 + 26 =	**39**
42 - 25 =	**17**	5 × 3 =	**15**

Page 144

		7					
		6					
				10			6
4	3						
				4	2		
2			3				
		8				3	
				6			

Page 145

Ice: office / icebox
Tan: suntan / tangoing
Thought: forethought / thoughtfully

Page 146

S	H	L	R	E	R	M	E	A	A	L	R	L	A	H
L	C	E	S	E	G	S	R	T	E	A	R	S	O	O
B	G	L	S	H	R	G	N	B	B	A	N	A	E	B
C	R	A	M	O	E	L	H	B	O	O	N	O	F	E
E	L	E	H	L	L	E	I	I	K	D	S	L	F	A
T	R	A	I	T	L	T	P	N	O	P	E	E	A	V
M	H	O	M	A	A	M	I	G	E	N	A	E	R	E
O	N	E	M	A	M	L	A	A	B	E	W	L	I	R
U	I	E	A	N	A	I	F	E	A	H	R	E	G	U
S	M	O	N	K	E	Y	A	P	E	R	H	P	C	C
E	R	A	L	L	I	R	O	G	E	M	R	H	S	A
D	I	E	E	E	N	A	R	M	S	I	L	A	A	M
B	Y	T	A	R	L	B	B	A	B	T	L	N	L	E
N	A	L	B	S	A	O	B	T	R	L	G	T	E	L
C	O	G	W	O	C	A	B	E	E	B	O	B	E	I

Page 147

5	54	15	30	10	**2**
77	49	42	41	85	**17**
472	118	177	59	365	**511**

Solutions

Page 148

	C		C		V		A	
	O		L		E	A	R	L
I	N	F	I	N	I	T	E	
	S	I	N		L	O	A	F
	T	R	I	P		M		L
	A		C		S	I	R	E
A	B	S		S		C	A	W
	L	E	E	K			N	
	E	N	V	I	S	A	G	E
		S	I	M	P	L	E	R
D	U	E	L		A	P	S	E

Page 149

Won, zloty, lira, dram, dollar, krone

Page 150

Aquarius, Sagittarius, Cassiopeia, Andromeda

Page 152

6	6	2	4	5	6	0	0
0	1	3	3	2	1	1	5
3	0	4	6	4	4	1	4
3	2	5	2	1	4	5	2
2	6	0	3	5	1	5	0
6	0	5	2	4	6	1	1
5	0	3	2	6	4	3	3

Page 153

Ireland, Australia, Portugal, Argentina, Germany

Page 154

Extreme, acquired, astronaut, brevity, exec

Page 155

SEEK › SEEN › TEEN › THEN › THIN › THIS

Page 156

50 = 17 + 19 + 14
70 = 9 + 33 + 28
90 = 24 + 29 + 37

Page 157

T	S	P	S	U	L	U	M	U	C	O	T	L	A	T
F	U	I	U	L	A	C	U	N	O	S	U	S	T	S
L	T	L	I	A	A	R	C	U	S	A	L	U	U	S
M	A	E	C	O	A	S	U	S	L	S	S	C	U	P
U	R	U	I	A	R	S	U	U	U	T	A	U	Y	C
U	T	S	S	T	S	R	U	T	L	P	U	R	T	S
F	S	T	I	U	R	T	A	T	O	L	O	U	S	N
E	O	U	P	I	N	R	E	A	A	C	A	U	I	V
O	R	T	C	A	T	I	S	L	U	L	C	L	E	U
U	R	S	L	S	S	U	C	M	L	N	U	L	L	I
I	I	U	O	T	S	S	U	N	I	A	U	D	T	C
S	C	T	I	P	U	L	I	U	U	M	N	S	N	N
O	L	U	L	T	U	E	S	S	N	U	E	U	U	U
A	L	E	L	S	S	U	T	A	R	B	I	F	S	N
M	A	L	I	N	T	O	R	T	U	S	T	N	A	S

Page 158

Detour	Routed
Drawer	Warred
Gaping	Paging
Groans	Organs
Leased	Sealed
Luring	Ruling
Meaner	Rename
Nested	Tensed
Neural	Unreal
Opuses	Spouse
Ouster	Routes
Palest	Staple
Panels	Planes
Panted	Pedant
Parses	Spares

Solutions

Page 159

Photosynthesises uses all the letters. Other words include hot, photo, photos, photosynthesis, photosynthesise, sis, sot, syntheses, synthesis, synthesise, synthesises, the, these, theses, thesis and thy

Page 160

					299					
				155		144				
			78		77		67			
		35		43		34		33		
	13		22		21		13		20	
6		7		15		6		7		13

Page 161

Deer	Reed
Spoons	Snoops
Stops	Spots
Warts	Straw

Page 162

There are 16 stars:

Page 163

H	A	M	■	P	A	R
I	■	I	R	E	■	A
P	O	X	■	R	O	T
■	■	T	■	F	■	■
T	A	U	■	U	R	N
O	■	R	A	M	■	O
G	E	E	■	E	A	R

Page 164

4		5	>	2	>	1		3
v								
2		3		5		4		1
5		2	>	1		3		4
						v		
3		1		4		2		5
								v
1		4	>	3		5		2

Page 165

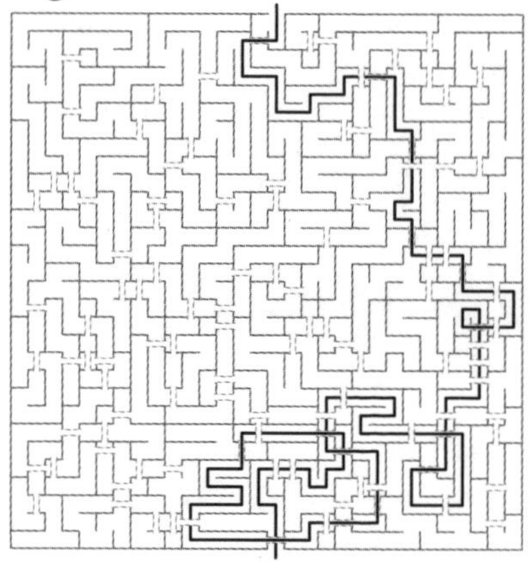

Solutions

Page 166

	E	V	E	N	S		P	L	A	C	E	D
R		I		I		B		I		O		O
I	N	T	E	R	P	R	E	T		N	E	E
N		A		V		I		H		C		S
S	A	L	S	A		D	E	E	M	E	D	
E				N		E				R		
	A	R	R	A	N	G	E	M	E	N	T	
		O				R		O				I
	S	T	U	D	I	O		M	E	E	T	S
T		A		A		O		E		A		L
W	E	T		R	E	M	I	N	I	S	C	E
E		E		T		S		T		E		T
E	L	D	E	S	T		A	S	I	D	E	

Page 167

Strawberry	Blackberry
Watermelon	Pomegranate
Banana	Lychee
Kiwi	Clementine
Raspberry	Lemon
Peach	Pear
Satsuma	Lime

Page 169

The Mindfulness Puzzle Book

From the same author,
Dr Gareth Moore

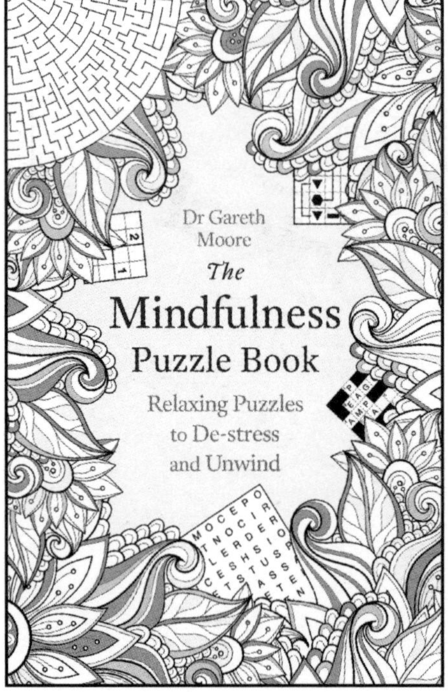

Enjoyed this book? Try the previous volume!

This book features a wide range of specially selected games to provide the perfect level of challenge and reward for your brain. Feel the tension release as you focus on each achievable and fun task, and experience the endorphin reward buzz as you successfully complete each puzzle.

Stimulating your mind with each puzzle helps unlock your brain's innate creativity, just as sleep and rest can help you reach a breakthrough on pending tasks. This book will help you feel refreshed and renewed, and ready to carry on with your daily life.

Puzzles include a wide selection of standard puzzle types, avoiding the stress of the new, but without the boredom of over-repetition. They also include adult versions of relaxing kids' activities, such as dot-to-dots, mazes and even colouring and spot-the-difference puzzles.

Visit www.littlebrown.co.uk for more information.

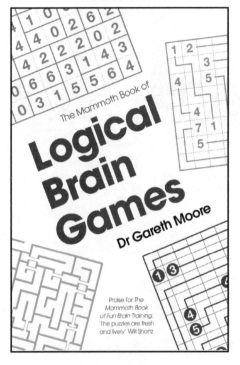

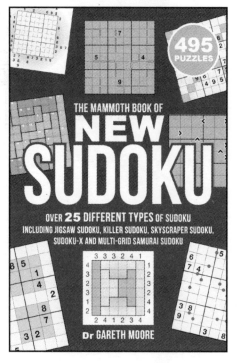